Elk Hunting 501
MAKING IT HAPPEN IN ELK COUNTRY

Jay Houston

www.ElkCamp.com
ElkCamp.com Outdoor Adventures

America's #1 Online Resource for Elk Hunters
Jackson Creek Publishers
Colorado Springs, Colorado 80920

ELK HUNTING 301
MAKING IT HAPPEN IN ELK COUNTRY

Jay Houston

Copyright 2006 by
Jay Houston / Author

Our magnificent front cover photo is courtesy of Jerry Gowins. Please see "About the Photographer" inside the book to learn more about Jerry and his work.

All rights reserved. No part of this publication may be reproduced, stored in a retrieval system, or transmitted in any form or by any means—electronic, mechanical, digital, photocopy, recording, or any other—except for brief quotations in printed reviews, without the prior written permission of the author and publisher.

Printed in the United States of America

ISBN 0-9759319-2-X

Jackson Creek Publishers
8697 Bellcove Circle
Colorado Springs, Colorado 80920

TABLE OF CONTENTS

Two Monster Bulls …Two Memories Up Close and Personal 7

Find the Food, Find the Elk 25

Elk Behavior…Understanding Why Elk Do What They Do 34

Elk Hunting Is Not A Spectator Sport 49

Locating Trophy Class Bulls 55

A Veteran Elk Hunter's Thoughts On Success 65

A Serious Bowhunter's Secrets to Success 71

Hunting With A Professional Outfitter… If There Is A Short Cut This May Be It 81

Tree Stands and Ground Blinds for Elk 87

Pass It On – The Next Generation 96

Thoughts From A Woman Hunter 109

A Country Elk Hunter Speaks 115

Quartering Your Elk Without Field Dressing 124

Hot New Gear For Elk Hunters 128

Join the Rocky Mountain Elk Foundation

Folks, whether you are an elk hunter or someone who just loves elk country, I genuinely want to encourage you to give serious consideration to becoming a member of the Rocky Mountain Elk Foundation. As a member for many years, I believe that no other single organization has done more for elk and elk country. If we want to preserve this wondrous resource for the generations to come, then we must choose to get involved personally and take measures to preserve the land that these magnificent creatures live in…i.e. we must become a part of "Making It Happen In Elk Country."

The mission of the Rocky Mountain Elk Foundation is to ensure the future of elk, other wildlife and their habitat. Folks, if you're serious about elk, this is not a difficult decision. You can make a difference. Please don't make the mistake of putting this decision off thinking someone else will step up to the plate. For our children and our grandchildren, this responsibility is yours and mine. Please join me in this most worthy endeavor. It is a small investment to make but the return will benefit countless generations of elk hunters and elk lovers to come. Just pick up the phone and dial **800-CALL-ELK** and join today.

My special thanks to the following first-rate folks on staff or volunteers with RMEF who directly or indirectly have helped to make our books and our efforts to have a constructive impact in the lives of those who travel the trails of elk country a success: J. Dart, Lance Schul, Dr. Terry Sweet, Troy Sweet, Don Burgess, Dan Crockett, Beth Shipley, Brandee Sperry, Erin DeGroot, Tamara McDermott, and Chris Croy.

Acknowledgements

First and foremost, I want to thank my wonderful wife, Rae Ann, for loving me endlessly, encouraging me daily, and blessing me with the freedom to share elk country with today's hunters and future generations.

Lance Schul, Senior Regional Director-Colorado for the Rocky Mountain Elk Foundation who has remained a true friend, consistent supporter and encourager as we have journeyed over many trails together. Thanks bro.

Vickie Gardner, of Alpen Optics who has never met a stranger and doesn't know how not to smile. Thanks Vickie for choosing to trust, support and befriend this writer. You are a grand friend, and a true lady of the outdoors.

Roger Medley, my faithful friend, brother-in-Christ, and huntin' buddy for his never-ending patience, solid advice, and years of encouragement.

J.R. Keller, a world-champion elk caller and elk hunter for his personal friendship, encouragement, and faithful professional support. A man who chose to make his family his first love. Way to go J.R!

Lew Claspell, a die-hard bowhunter, friend and neighbor. Few will go farther or hunt harder in pursuit of these awe-inspiring creatures. Lew, thanks for your friendship and for your generous contribution to this work.

Randy Matthews, a world-class father and husband, a true brother-in-Christ, former pro shooter turned real bowhunter, and a man with a passion for passing it on to future generations. For your unending support, friendship, and contribution to this work, thanks Randy.

ELK HUNTING 301…Making It Happen In Elk Country

Forward

Learning is a lifelong experience and we consider it an honor to have this opportunity to come along side you for a while. Our hope is that some of what you read within will end up in your next elk hunting play book thus helping to better equip you for this path along your life's journey. Rather than produce a massive 400-page book that you will never take to camp and that might end up gathering dust on some shelf, we have chosen to share this information with you in smaller yet more digestible bites, i.e. three separate books presented over time. If you missed our first two books, then you have missed two-thirds of the story. I would encourage you to seek out copies of Elk Hunting 101 and Elk Hunting 201 from our website, www.ElkCamp.com, www.amazon.com, or your local bookstore. If you cannot find a copy on the shelf, ask a sales clerk to order it for you.

In this volume we have included essays by a few of our very special hunting buddies who we believe have valuable insight to share with you. Each writer offers a unique, insightful, and even colorful approach to the subject of elk hunting. One of our favorite women hunters as well as a few younger elk hunters particularly honored us by contributing their work to this effort. We hope you enjoy their contributions, as they are integral to the purpose of Elk Hunting 301.

Our desire is to help educate you by providing you with practical, field-tested, well-researched accurate information. If along the way we help prepare you for your next great hunt and all the future opportunities that you may encounter in elk country, then we consider our efforts a success.

Rae Ann and I hope you benefit from the read. Our prayer is that God will richly bless you and that you will enjoy the journey in elk country.

Jay

Chapter One

Two Monster Bulls ... Two Memories Up Close and Personal

Four of us were dead-tired and crashed in a blow-down midway down the slope of one of the steepest and most treacherous mountainsides that I had ever hunted. My hunting partners for the week, TJ Shiimunek, host of Gammy Creek Outdoors TV, his videographer Pat Walderzak, guide Brian Parks of Centennial Trail Outfitters and I were surrounded by an impenetrable forest of ancient western red Cedars, many towering well beyond the one-hundred foot mark, and Alders so thick that horizontal visibility was often limited to ten feet or less. Our small band of hunters was recuperating after spending four exhausting hours with our noses to the ground tracking the blood trail of a monster bull that had been arrowed two days earlier on the other side of the mountain by TJ's business partner Zach Poff. To say we were all tired would have been nothing short of gross sarcasm. One look at our motley crew with our bows and gear scattered about the forest floor would not have led one to believe that we were in pursuit of anything more than a good nap.

Each of us had come to Idaho in September of 2005 with dreams of arrowing a 300-class or better P&Y bull. However, monster bulls were the farthest things from our minds during these few moments of respite.

As I half dozed with my back up against a fallen Cedar and Idaho bulls the last thing on my mind, I noticed Pat out of the corner of my eye sit up and reach for his camera while slowly turning his head in my direction. To my amazement his eyes were as wide as saucers and all he could manage to whisper were three brief words that would trigger the beginning of an elk country encounter that I will treasure for the rest of my life, those words were "Bull... Big Bull." And then...all you-know-what broke loose.

Sixteen years of pursuing these majestic antlered beasts throughout my home state of Colorado, mostly as a rifle hunter, could never have prepared me for what would happen next and how fast it would all come together.

For those of you who have experienced such an up-close encounter, you will probably empathize with me as I recall some of the many thoughts that passed through my brain literally in a matter of seconds. Don't move too quickly... move your eyes first not your head...identify the clear shooting lanes...where is the wind...are there cows close by that can bust me...where will the bull appear...make sure that the angle to the target is good...don't look at the rack...focus on a small two-inch spot behind the shoulder...don't look at the rack fool...what's the range to the primary shooting lane...20 yards...what's the range to the back up lane...25 yards...which pin is the correct pin...the green pin...no the yellow pin...no the green 20 yard pin with a little adjustment...yep...does the vertical angle to the target require a range adjustment...nope not enough to worry about...check the wind again...don't look at the rack...and on it went. Breathe calmly...think back position...shoulder position...wrist...breathe again...finger behind the trigger of the release...draw...anchor...now finger around the trigger...don't punch it...take your time...clear the target area...ok now don't breathe...focus...take your time...where are the shakes...there are supposed to be shakes...just a little back pressure for the shot. Focus on the small spot.

As the shooter with the honors, I ever-so-slowly reached for my PSE Vengeance bow that was leaning against a fallen log just an arm's length away, while moving my eyes in the direction where all the commotion was coming from. For those interested, I was packing Easton Axis ST 400s and NAP 100 grain Nitron broadheads.

As I strained to see through the dense undergrowth, a thunderous bawl that literally made the hair on the back of my neck stand straight up erupted just forty yards out from our hideaway. Within seconds the ivory-tipped rack of a monster bull that was more than wide enough to bracket the top of a VW bug began to magically appear a few inches at a time coming up the side of the bench where we were hiding in the dense Cedar and Alders. Having just snatched two cows from an even larger bull that we had named the Growler far down the mountain, this bruiser was really full of himself, screaming as he shredded limbs from a three-inch Cedar two at a time. To say the least there was no shortage of testosterone and this big boy was really worked up. Thus, after three days of some of the toughest, sometimes near vertical, high country hunting I had ever experienced, all of my instincts, knowledge, skill, and practice came online and kicked into high gear telling me that it was now time to get down to business.

My first Idaho bowhunt had its beginnings four months earlier, when I was contacted by Kevin Paulson and Randy Parks, co-owners of Centennial Trail Outfitters (CTO) about the possibility of my helping them book elk, mule deer, and bear hunters for their outfit. Kevin shared with me that one of their permitted areas held some very nice bulls and that they wanted my help through our business ElkCamp.com Outdoor Adventures in booking some additional hunters.

Having developed a reputation as a reliable elk-hunting consultant over the past ten years, I have a firm rule that requires that I hunt with any prospective new outfitter or landowner before I will recommend their services to one of our clients. Experience has taught me that any outfit can sound good, but the one true test of the quality and integrity of an outfitting business is to spend time in ElkCamp hunting with them. I shared this with Kevin and all he said was, "When do you want to come out and hunt?" My 2005 hunting season was already pretty full with a Colorado rifle elk hunt in mid-October and an Ohio bowhunt for whitetail in late October-early November, but the opportunity to get on what I hoped would be a 300-class or better bull with a bow was just too much to pass up. I made a few calls and called Kevin back to tell him that I would arrive on September 14th.

Due to the extreme amount of hunting pressure on public land in my home state of Colorado, I usually council my hunting clients to seriously consider taking the first legal animal that they have a good shot at. However, since Randy had told me that his area had more than its share of 300-class or better bulls, I set my standards for this hunt a bit higher.

Come what may, it would be a 300 plus class bull or nothing for me on this particular hunt.

After flying into Spokane, Randy picked me the following morning and we began the two-hour drive back to his ranch near St. Regis, Montana. We talked about elk hunting, guiding, my books, our families and a lot of that first contact small talk that occurs in such situations as two strangers are trying to get to know one another. As we were going back though our respective life histories, a number of similarities in our individual journeys began to be revealed. As a Christian I have never been one to believe in coincidence, but more so in what I like to call Divine Appointments. The more we shared, the more it became apparent that our meeting was looking more like a Divine Appointment. Randy would share something and I would say, "You've got to be kidding me, me too!" I would share a story and Randy would say the same thing. Here we were, driving up a mountain in the wilds of Idaho, miles from anywhere, each sitting next to who we thought was a perfect stranger. As the stories flowed however the truth of this rendezvous began to unfold. Randy and I had grown up together, playing on the same little league ball team, attending the same church, and even having the same piano teacher as young boys in Memphis. Finally, I couldn't take the suspense any longer and asked Randy if he had a brother. He says sure, Mike. "Mike Parks" I said, "You're Mike's brother?" It was as if forty years of history had been folded back and I was twelve years old again. After forty years, separate lives, thousands of miles, families, and careers, God had chosen to reunite two long lost boyhood friends high on a mountain in Idaho. While I didn't show it, my heart was crying out at God's amazing reunion of two good friends, each forgotten from so long ago.

I have always believed that if one wants to hunt really fired-up bulls during the rut, the last two weeks of September can often be your best bet. Accordingly, I was not surprised when the rut in the area around our camp started to gain momentum on September 15th, our first day out, and then kicked into high gear two days later with bulls going nuts and bugling all over the range that we were hunting.

Mid-morning on the second day found one of my hunting partners Zach Poff and his videographer Ryan Themm (that's camera guy to most of us but they like to be called videographers) about 900 feet up a steep Alder and Cedar slope above a bowl that was known to hold a heavily beamed 6x6 bull. The word from our guides was that each morning the bull would climb out of the hole that he spent the night in using a known route to cross the higher ridge above the bowl through a saddle. Zach and Ryan had left camp far before daybreak with a plan to waylay this bruiser as he made his way towards his bedding area on the opposite side of the saddle.

As it so often happens in elk country, the elk fail to read our playbook and come up with some pretty surprising plays of their own. Expecting the big six-by to be coming up the slope from the bowl below, Zach and Ryan set up accordingly with Ryan playing the role of both videographer and caller. Ryan began by making a few brief high-pitched bugles imitating an immature bull followed by a series of estrus cow calls, a strategy frequently used to rile up a more mature bull by making him think that there is a young bull nearby with a few cows tagging along. Almost immediately a bull responded to Ryan's calls, not from down the ridge as expected, but from up the mountain. Score so far, Elk 1, Hunters 0.

According to Zach and Ryan this bad boy was madder than a thousand hornets at the thought of another bull having snuck into his territory, and he was determined to let someone know just how ticked off he was. Zach and Ryan decided to quickly swap positions so that Ryan would be calling from behind Zach who was now the uphill member of the team.

No sooner had they swapped positions than the bull appeared, working his way through the Alders with fire in his eyes looking to pick a fight with the intruder bull that he had just heard. Now the pace was picking up. So as not to be detected, Zach drew his bow when the bull was looking away and then he knelt below a small Alder bush. Having seen the video of this encounter, Zach must have felt like he was at full draw forever, but in reality it was only a few seconds before the bull was on him...literally.

Zach Poff & "The Bull Coming In"   Still shot from video

The monster bull had come in quickly and stopped a mere five feet from where Zach was hidden at full draw beneath the Alders that were directly under the bull's neck and chest. I wish I could say that with my forty years of big game hunting experience that I could have been as cool and collected as a twenty-five year old Zach was, but I seriously doubt that I would have had half the control that this younger hunter showed under such extreme circumstances. Way to go Zach! Had it been me, there might have been a change of clothes required after such a close encounter. According to Zach, a number of things were going through his mind as he hid beneath this enormous bull that was all but drooling on his cap, not the least of which was the very real possibility of getting stomped or even gored if the bull discovered him. With no five-foot pin on his sight, Zach waited until the bull looked over him for the other elusive bull before placing his entire sight pin guard on the bull's vitals just feet away. After the fact, Zach told us that before the shot he wasn't even sure if the arrow would clear the bow before it hit the bull. But clear the bow it did. Though the shaft didn't have time to achieve maximum velocity it had plenty of juice to bury itself all the way up to the vanes in the bulls vitals.

Following the shot, the confused bull bolted from sight and disappeared back into the impenetrable brush as quickly as he had come. Meanwhile Zach and Ryan collapsed and tried to recover from what would likely be the closest encounter of their lives with the bull of a lifetime.

At about the same time, my guide Brian Parks and I were on the opposite side of the same mountain. We had scrambled one foot at a time about a thousand feet up a killer grade that was near fifty degrees (vertical) in some places. Often times we would have to hold on to Alder limbs and literally swing from bush to bush to keep from rolling back down the mountain. To cover the racket that our trek was making we would make cow calls from time to time tossing in a bugle for good measure here and there. Brian was packing a Terminator bugle that was so powerful that it literally hurt my ears when he cut loose with it, and since the rut had hardly had time to build up much steam it wasn't producing much results. I asked Brian if he would mind if I tried a couple from my smaller Pack bugle, which imitates a much younger and less mature bull. He said, "You wrote the book, sure go for it." I laughed and just shook my head knowing that he was really just having a little fun at my expense. I whipped out the Pack Bugle™ and did my best to sound like some worked up but youthful bull looking for love. My first attempt produced the same results as that of Brian's Terminator…nada. Every instinct in me however, told me that the rut should be on, so why were the bulls being so quiet? I wondered. I waited about two minutes and let go with a second short bugle and before I had finished chuckling, two bulls quickly responded from nearby up hill. These boys were close. Their bugles seemed to surround us echoing off trees and undergrowth. The dark timber was so thick it was hard to tell exactly how far away the bulls were. Brian told me that in such thick timber the elk are usually closer than you think, so we estimated that the bull directly uphill was around sixty yards out, and the bull at our two o'clock was probably more like seventy-five yards away. Based on the varying volume of his bugles, we determined the uphill bull was probably working back and forth along a game trail that Brian knew of. The other bull was showing less interest, probably because he was a younger bull and didn't want any part of what was going on over our way.

The underbrush was too thick and the slope too steep to try a sneak. So for what seemed like the next half hour, Brian and I tried every call and trick in the book to lure one of these bulls down to us for a shot, but they were not going to have any of it. Since we didn't hear any cows, we assumed that while their testosterone was on the rise, it had not yet hit the point where either bull was ready for a real fight. Though we were not able to close the deal on these bulls, the adventure sure started my blood flowing and I realized that the hunt had only just begun.

With bulls beginning to bugle all around us as well as the other hunters in camp, we decided to try to hook up with the rest of our group and develop some sort of plan rather than to continue to bust brush at random. This can be a real challenge, especially if you're hunting with strangers who do not have foreknowledge of each other's skills and abilities. The temptation is for each hunter or hunting team to head off in random directions. However years of experience has taught me that working together with a plan almost always produces better results in the long run. So we headed back to camp to develop a group strategy.

Soon after arriving at camp, Zach and Ryan walked in with the "agony and ecstasy" tale of their close encounter, all of which was caught on videotape. Following the shot Zach and Ryan had waited for the bull to lie down. After what they thought was a respectable wait they set off along a spotty blood trail.

Time out from the story folks: I want to take this brief opportunity to talk about how long should you wait following the shot to pursue your animal, especially for Bowhunters. Elk are large bodied animals that in most cases when hit will only run a short distance after being shot whether with a rifle or bow before stopping to assess their situation. By this I don't mean to imply that they think it through, but more so their instinctive response is to flee the immediate area where they encountered a threat. Once clear, and this may be as few as fifty yards or so, if left alone and not pursued, they will slow down or stop. I like to cow call following the shot as a way to help a wounded animal to settle down. The tendency of most hunters that I have known or met is to wait a few minutes and then set off in pursuit of their trophy. Folks, each situation is different, but I can say with assurance that the hunter who pursues his elk prematurely is not going to get him to crash any sooner. Think about it, if someone had shot you and was chasing you with a gun or bow, would you stop to see what was going to happen?

Here are my rules of thumb for how long to wait. If the bull goes down right in front of me like he was pole-axed, I give him thirty minutes no questions asked before I move in his direction. If he runs out of sight following the shot, but I know with absolute certainty that he is hit hard in both lungs or the heart, I will wait anywhere from one to three hours. Finally, if there is any question in my mind, ANY, especially if

I'm bowhunting, that the shot was not a double lung or heart shot, I wait eight or more hours before pursuing the animal, the idea being to give the animal the opportunity to lie down and expire. When hit, the animal's body begins to flood with adrenaline to support his 'fight or flight mechanism.' Think of adrenaline like nitrous oxide, a fuel additive for racecars that when injected into the fuel stream substantially increases their horsepower and speed almost instantaneously. Once the adrenaline hits, the animal will use this increased fuel and horsepower to put as much distance between it and the threat it perceives, until either the fuel runs out, or it no longer perceives the threat. I have heard stories of more animals lost forever because the hunter could not wait to get on the move to see what he had shot, and the animal kept moving, though mortally wounded, for miles. Patience is the key folks.

Back to the story: Seeing bubbles in the blood Zach was sure that his arrow had taken out at least one of the bull's lungs and that he wouldn't be able to go far and must have crashed nearby in the thick brush. After hours of scouring the mountain for Zach's bull to no avail, they decided to return to camp for more help.

Since Ryan had captured the entire event on videotape, each of us took our turn watching the event unfold through the camera's small viewfinder. When the tape came to the part with the monster bull almost standing over Zach, looking directly over his head as Zach remained frozen at full draw in the brush, all you could hear was, "You've gotta be kidding me!" Well that's sort of what they said.

With a wounded bull on the mountain it was agreed upon that we should focus on recovering the bull. So for the better part of that afternoon and most of the following morning teams of hunters, packers, and guides combed nearly every inch of the mountainside where Ryan had taken his shot, but in the end…no bull.

The afternoon following Ryan's encounter TJ, Pat, my guide Brian and I set off for the top of the mountain in hopes of locating another shooter bull. Upon reaching the summit we were treated to one of the most spectacular views of the hunt, as we were able to take in hundreds of square miles of mountains and timber. We spent a few extra minutes on the summit taking pictures and then headed off down the mountain in search of Mr. Big.

After about an hour of working our way diagonally across the slope we decided to set up and glass the draw below us. We knew that a good water source ran down the middle of the draw and hoped that the protection provided by the steep slopes on both sides and the water would hold elk. After glassing for about ten minutes, I bugled briefly to determine if perhaps anyone was home. Almost immediately the deep raspy bugle of a mature bull answered my bugle from far below. I bugled back. This conversation back and forth continued for about half an hour. I could tell by the change in this monster's tone that he was moving back and forth along a line running from us to him. My guess was that he had cows with him and that when he would come to our end of the herd, a satellite bull would try to come in from the other end and try to cut out some of his cows so he would charge back the other way. Sitting on the bluff we had heard the second bull on and off as we called. Knowing that we would not be able to make it down to the bull with the wind in our favor before dark, we decided to leave and come back the next morning hoping to approach the bull from a different angle and make a close approach with the wind in our favor. As we gathered our gear and got up to leave the area someone said, "that bull sure does growl at lot." Thus we named this bull appropriately...the Growler.

That evening we made a plan to have the packers drop us off at the top of the mountain early the next morning. They would then return to camp and take a truck and park it across the river at the base of the mountain. We would hunt down the mountain throughout the next day crossing the river and taking the truck back to camp that night. Knowing that our departure the next morning would come far too soon, we all ate quickly and called it an early night. With visions of the Growler dancing in all of our heads, needless to say sleep did not come easily for at least one of us...me.

The following morning dawned chilly with a bit of fog floating in the deep mountain valleys like a downy blanket with holes all over the place and mountaintops poking through. The upper slopes of the mountain were steep, so we elected to wait at the top until it was light enough to see without flashlights to begin our trek down to the Growler. As we made our trek down we began to hear two bulls bugling back and forth, coming from far below, but it was clear that neither of these was the Growler. Both sounded like younger bulls. Sometimes however, bugles will fool you and you can end up with a mature bull in your lap thinking it is a raghorn coming in. The Cedar and Alders were thick so it was difficult to tell how far away these bulls were. Occasionally we would cow call just to keep their attention. On two separate occasions, we thought one or the other of the bulls was coming in and set up, only to have the setup blown by swirling winds each time. The four of us worked the two bulls for about an hour with no luck before moving on down the mountain.

As we were making our way through some underbrush we came across a blood trail that appeared to be less than 24 hours old. Determining the age of a blood trail can be difficult if there has been rain, or moisture in the air that keeps the blood wet. Though we were not certain as to its age, we set off on the trail anyway. Early on the trail was fairly clear and consistent and appeared to have come from the top of the mountain along a route that paralleled the one we had taken. We quickly surmised that this might be the trail of

Zach's bull, so for the next four hours our gang of scruffy camo-clad warriors put our hunt on hold and took to the trail like a pack of Tennessee Bloodhounds. Knowing that there was good water at the bottom and that wounded animals often try to make their way to a water source, we were fairly certain where this bull was going. It was just a matter of staying with the trail until we caught up with the bull. Many times we would loose the trail in the heavy brush, only to pick it up again. Unfortunately however, the trail ended in a Cedar thicket near a big blood blowout. We couldn't figure out how the bull could have made it past this point with so much loss of blood, but this blood didn't have the frothy look of the blood near where Zach took his shot. This blood was much darker with very little froth. My guess is that Zach's shot may have missed the near lung and either clipped the far lung or more than likely hit the liver. Either way, this bull had come a long way. Eventually we all agreed that there was not much hope in finding the bull, so we rejoined our hunt for the Growler farther down the mountain. By this time we were all pretty tired from the tracking so we decided to take a short break and grab a bite to eat in a sunny little blow-down on a small bench and it was here that my encounter with the broad beamed bull exploded.

In my years of elk hunting I have seen quite a few bulls with more mass than this fellow, but none with such an expansive outside spread from antler tip to tip. The main beams of most bulls leave the skull at an upturned angle, this monster's rack turned almost ninety-degrees to the left and right before sweeping to the vertical.

As I mentioned earlier, this bull was making his way up the mountain at a pretty good clip with two cows that he had just hijacked from another bull…probably the Growler down below. The cows were in the lead and I really didn't want to blow this deal and get busted by one of the cows while drawing my bow before the bull stepped into a good shooting

ELK HUNTING 301…Making It Happen In Elk Country

lane. Since I could clearly see the cows moving up the hill, I assumed that they would see me draw so I held off, waiting for them to move on past me and back into the Alder brush. All the while a bull of a lifetime is getting closer and closer trying to catch up to his cows. I picked out what I thought would be the perfect shooting lane that would provide me with a broadside shot at 20 yards (no time for a rangefinder) if the bull cooperated. I came to full draw just prior to the bull stepping into the lane, but as I was starting to settle the pin behind his shoulder, the bull made an abrupt turn to his left to get around a tree leaving me with nothing but a tail on shot which I wouldn't take. Immediately I began searching for another clear shooting lane. As the bull was constantly weaving through the thick undergrowth, it was nearly impossible to predict where he would next pop out into the clear. Still at full draw, I'm watching the bull work his way around a couple of Cedars, while at the same time trying to mentally range a small opening where I think he will come into the clear. Finally, the bull stepped into a small lane but he was lower than I anticipated. He must have stepped into a shallow depression, which lowered his body with respect to the ground between us. I knew I had only a second to make the decision. I mentally estimated the range to be twenty-five yards. Settling the twenty-yard pin to compensate for the downward angle of the shot just behind the shoulder, I released.

To this day, I can still mentally envision the scene playing out in slow motion frame by frame. The bull is momentarily frozen with his head turned looking straight at me trying to make sense of this camo-clad image before him, the black Easton Axis arrow with a white wrap and white vanes is tracking directly towards the bull for a perfect double lung shot. My eyes move to those of the bull. I can without a doubt see something register in his eyes as they grow wider yet still focused on me that all is not right but he cannot figure it out so he remains steady. Again my eye picks up the white vanes still in flight...closer now but still on track. Then it happens. The arrow disappears. No warning, no nothing. It's there one second and gone the next. My ear detects the whack of a solid hit and the bull whirls and crashes back down the mountain. It's over...but what is over?

Now the adrenaline hits. My mind races, how far will he go? How are we going to get him out of this, the most desolate of places? Did Pat get the shot on tape? Now TJ is rushing over with high-fives. Everyone is pumped...especially me. With about a gallon of adrenaline now rushing through my veins like it was shot out of a fire hose, I cannot even manage to hit TJ's hand with a return to his high-five. Air...where did all the air go. I am caught up in the rush of the event! Thirty seconds ago I was almost asleep, now this. Then comes the news that none of us expected or wanted to hear. Pat has rewound the videotape and thinks that there may have been a problem with the shot. No...that's not possible. I had seen the arrow mere feet from the bull's vitals still on track. I heard the whack of impact. How could this be? As Pat studies the videotape, TJ walks over to where the bull was standing and discovers the truth. There, imbedded in a log lay my perfectly clean arrow. A few feet short of where the bull had stood just a few minutes before was the answer to the mystery. The small nearly invisible yet neatly severed stem that my arrow had inadvertently struck on its way to the bull's vitals.

ELK HUNTING 301...Making It Happen In Elk Country

The author's ecstasy before the agony   Still shot from video

Rags to riches, victory and defeat, life and death, often it seems that mere seconds are all that stand between the two. In this instance I was unable to close the deal successfully. However, I experienced one of the most remarkable hunts of my life. I now have a memory that I can playback over and over again reliving every heart-pounding second, any time I choose. Traveling around the country speaking at shows and hunting events I tell this story time and again. And every time I get the same response...what an opportunity! What a hunt!

I took the time to include this story in this book for two reasons. First to reinforce that fact that I believe that elk hunting is more about the experience than the end result. It is about the challenges of the journey from valley floor to mountaintop. It is about being witness to and participant in a legacy passed down to each of us by our fathers and their fathers. Hunting joins us together in one of God's greatest creations...Elk Country. The second reason I include this tale of the most physically challenging hunt of my life at age 52 is to emphasize the importance of becoming "a true hunter." Well...I am a hunter you may say. What is he talking about? I mean that in seventeen years of elk hunting I have been witness to many 'wannabe' hunters who I can only describe as folks casually taking their rifle or bow for a stroll in the woods, who I am sure are not having the type of hunt that they desire. Are these the hunters who regularly have elk back straps for supper, or at least get to experience moments like those in the story just told? In all honesty…probably not.

So what's the difference between those who consistently have opportunities like the one I shared, and those who do not? You have to be willing to do whatever it takes, to go the extra mile. You must have the knowledge, the confidence, the gear, the skill, the perseverance, and the internal drive to Make It Happen…In Elk Country.

You know what, that bruiser bull is still out there, and I will soon be returning to that Idaho elk country. He and I have another date, and I intend to be there for the dance.

Three twenty-something's, fine men & elk hunters that challenged the author up and down big mountains for a week in Idaho, 2005.
Brian Parks, Pat Walderzak, and T.J Shiimunek

Chapter Two

Find the Food, Find the Elk

Experienced elk hunters, terrestrial biologists, DNR type folks, and this writer agree, the number one item on an elk's checklist of priorities is locating and consuming food of the highest nutritional quality available. Ninety percent of an elk's day is consumed with feeding and resting. While other needs may rank high, absolutely nothing supersedes an elk's dietary requirements. Not security and not breeding...survival is about food. Without the essential nutrition elk acquire by feeding, all else is pretty much a moot point. If you are serious about elk hunting, you should get serious on learning about their feeding habits.

When I began my research for the subject matter that would eventually become "the meat and potatoes" of this book, I decided to do something different, I pulled out my entire library of elk hunting literature, books, magazines, journals, everything. I didn't have any idea how much of this stuff I had until it was all there in the middle of my office floor, stacks and stacks, piles upon piles. Then I began to search out the critical information that was missing or only minimally addressed in the literature. To my surprise, at the top of the list were elk feeding habits. I thought, how could such an essential topic manage to acquire so little attention? Like humans and all other creatures elk require fuel [food] to exist. Cell generation and repair, respiration, circulation, propagation, gestation, survival, fight or flight, each aspect of existence requires fuel to function. Nutrition is the key ingredient to survival.

In all the years that I have been elk hunting, I have yet to knowingly run into a hunter in the field that could tell me, by name and sight, which plant that elk prefer to feed on. While I am sure that there are many hunters that do possess this information, I offer that they may be the exception rather than the rule. Therefore this discussion will focus on elk feeding habits, including the differences between the feeding habits of bull and cow elk. By understanding the specifics of how and why elk feed as they do, it should lead us to a better understanding of the elk, which hopefully will allow us as hunters to better predict where elk will be at a given time.

When planning a future hunt the smart hunter should factor into the plan two established aspects of elk behavior. First, elk are exceedingly opportunistic, meaning that they are adaptable and will whenever possible take advantage of favorable situations. It is this opportunism that has caused elk to become such a migratory creature seizing upon a variety of food sources. How does this play out for the hunter?

ELK HUNTING 301…Making It Happen In Elk Country

In the fall as forage with the high nutritional value elk require to make it through the rut and the following winter months becomes more and more scarce, the elk are motivated to continually travel to new growth food sources as they become available. They will exploit these until the food source is depleted or other factors such as extreme weather or predators force them to move on. Sources of new growth forage change as seasons progress from late August into the early winter months. In late August and early September, new growth can still be found throughout most elk summer range in open grasslands, moist secluded forests, near valley floor seeps, and along water sources near the heads of drainages. It is this broad dispersal of food sources with a high nutritional value that factors into why elk may be in a particular drainage today and in another drainage tomorrow.

Once the frosts of mid to late September begin to take their toll on the quality of food in a particular area, the elk will move again in search of quality forage. When adverse weather, either too warm or too cold, moves into the area, elk herds usually break into smaller groups and will quickly seek the late season new growth and security that can be found on the forest floor in heavily timbered tracts which also offer a protective thermal barrier from the effects of the weather. This shift from open area grazing to forests is usually abrupt because it typically coincides with the beginning of hunting season. While hunting pressure is a factor in the transition, research indicates that this movement is related more to the availability of forage with high nutritional value and changes in temperature. As freezing nights take their toll on grassland food sources, the elk will transition from graze to browse and their use of forested areas will increase. Concurrent with the onset of hunting seasons is the rut, which throws a wrench into the normal foraging patterns of the elk. Bulls and cows alike are required to put reproduction on the front burner for a short period of time. It is during the rut that bulls may burn off as much as thirty percent of their accumulated body fat herding and breeding, leaving them in a severely energy depleted state going into winter.

Sparring bulls during the rut   Photo - Vince Martinez

Following the rut, with the possible exception of a few younger bulls, the cows and bulls begin to separate. Studies suggest that it is the bulls that choose to leave the cows. Factors that influence this decision are that bulls, having expended large amounts of energy, must make the most of the time remaining to build fat stores before the deep snows of winter arrive. To avoid competing for essential forage with the cows whose reproductive priorities are to optimize security for calves over quality forage; the bulls depart the herd for areas where competition is less. Larger more mature herd bulls that have expended more of their energy and fat reserves usually seek the best opportunities they can find for food as well as refuge from hunters in secluded forested tracts at the highest elevations. Another factor for this dispersal of cows and bulls is predation. As the snow level gets deeper in the high country an elk's ability to flee is impaired and antlered bulls in a herd of cows easily stand out to predators, thus by remaining with the herd they risk becoming a target, especially older bulls. By separating from the cows and seeking out more secluded feeding and bedding areas, the bulls feel more secure.

Secondly, the lives of elk revolve around what Thomas & Toweill in their 1982 volume, *Elk of North America; Ecology and Management* refer to as the Law of Least Effort. This means that the necessary resources that elk require must be obtained with a minimum of effort in order to maximize the benefits derived. This rule is predominant in elk behavior and is evidenced by the amount of time elk invest in eating and resting as discussed earlier. The balance of their day, ten percent or less, is spent standing and walking around usually in close proximity to their bedding areas, the objective being to store up as much energy and fat as possible, while burning minimal calories. Elk behavior in winter such as walking one behind another in deep snow, feeding in softer shallow snow, or migrating to lower areas where they do not have to work as hard to feed are evidence of this.

I admit that for years I failed to give much attention to the differences in the feeding patterns of cow elk and those of bulls. In most cases during the hunting season, when we ran into a mixed herd of elk, i.e. cows and bulls, I was more focused on getting setup for a shot, and never gave their feeding habits a second thought. In recent years, however, with the heavy increases in hunting pressure on public lands, finding the elk has become the #1 challenge. Like most hunters, when the elk appeared to become scarce, we applied what might be called a brute force strategy, i.e. hunt harder and hunt longer. Unfortunately this strategy failed to produce the expected result. It was this failed strategy that I have witnessed or learned from year after year in camp after camp that brought me to the point of examining how most elk hunters hunt and what can be done to help them become more successful.

As a professional hunting consultant, writer and conference speaker on elk hunting, I have access to some of the best minds in the industry, from which I gather essential information on elk, elk hunting, and elk country. From guides and outfitters, to professional hunters, elk biologists, game managers, wildlife officers, and others, the answer to my search for a better strategy was the same: if you want to get into the elk, you have to hunt smarter! If we want to become more successful elk hunters in an ever-increasing environment of high-pressured elk, we will have to learn more about the elk themselves.

Dissimilar Feeding Habits of Bulls and Cows
So how is a cow's feeding different from that of a bull? Due the cow's role in reproduction, cow elk have an enhanced ability to acquire and store fat and nutrients from the forage they feed on during summer and fall. As a result of her increased ability to store fat and nutrients, the cow is not as dependent on high quality feed and thus can ingest more fibrous material than a bull during long winter months and is not as pressured to continually seek out new high quality food sources. Also because of her reserves, she will not have to feed as much or as often in winter. Not having to focus as much on forage, a cow's time is spent more on protecting her calf from predators. Large cow-calf herds that gather for mutual security and are observed in elk country throughout the winter evidence this.

Bulls on the other hand, especially the older mature bulls sought after by hunters, must pack away all the high quality nutrients they can find. The average bull will consume as much as twelve pounds of forage per day. If he hopes to survive the extreme temperatures found in elk country in winter, avoid predators, and play his role in maintaining the gene pool, he must focus his post rut efforts on maximizing his intake while minimizing his exertion.... again the law of least effort. As a vital player in the future of the gene pool, he must not compete with the cows that are responsible for producing and protecting the next generation. Due to his larger body size and antlers, the bull can afford to trade off security for forage. Soon after the end of the rut, the bulls begin to drift away from the cow-calf herd in search of sources of nutrient rich food. Less mature bulls may be found in small bachelor groups again as they were in summer if the forage is plentiful, but older larger bulls become quite solitary and reclusive.

Larger bulls become solitary after the rut.   Photo - Jerry Gowins

Because of their larger body size and its ability to absorb more heat, bulls must disperse significantly more retained heat than cows. This requirement causes bulls to seek out cooler areas in which to feed and rest such as dark timber, blow downs, and shadier North facing slopes on warmer days or days of bright sun. Typically larger bulls are the last to evacuate the cooler high country when winter snows begin to accumulate.

I have often been asked, "How much snow does it take to move elk out of the high country?" My hip pocket response is that when the snow depth begins to come up to an elk's belly, they start looking for an easier place to find lunch. For cow elk this may be 14 to 18 inches while for bulls it may take as much as 24 inches of snow to move them to another area. Keep in mind that there are no hard and fast numbers on this and that other factors may affect when elk begin to move down the mountain in search of an easier to obtain meal.

Hunting Burns
When it comes to the types of habitat in which we as hunters can expect to locate elk one that seems to cause a fair amount of discussion is that of small burns, i.e. areas that have been burned over in a past forest fire. Burns can play a vital role in the ecosystem for elk, thought perhaps not as vital for cows as for bulls. Nutrient rich forage in burn areas can begin to reappear in only a few months following a fire. The tender new shoots tend to attract elk for as much as three years following the fire. Small burns offer bulls a source of quality nutrients for building fat reserves and minerals for antler development during the summer. In fall these same areas provide excellent forage that help bulls make it through the winter. Because of the open area herding behavior as a form of protection against predators, cow elk do not frequent small burns as much as bulls.

Time spent feeding and bedding represents roughly 90% of an elk's (24 hour) day with prime daytime time feeding for elk coming in the first few hours after sunrise and the last few hours before sunset, while bedding takes up the majority of the time in-between. This schedule changes dramatically, however, during the rut. As both cows and bulls are focused on reproducing, much of the time otherwise used for bedding is now spent traveling or standing. Feeding continues to take up the lion's share of a 24-hour period, but rutting and rut related activity seems to override the need for sleep, especially for bulls. In the normal course of a 24-hour period, elk will feed and bed both day and night. During summer months the feeding patterns of elk remain about the same with regard to daytime or nighttime feeding, however the amount of time that they spend bedding at night almost doubles from 20 to 40% in winter as the elk attempt to optimize the use of every available calorie…again… the law of least effort.

Chapter Three

Elk Behavior…Understanding Why Elk Do What They Do

Bugling…What's That All About
Not too long ago I was bowhunting a steep brushy slope in Northern Idaho when out of nowhere and without the least bit of warning my hunting partner and I were enveloped by what I can only describe as a raspy guttural roaring from somewhere real close by. As the shear volume of sound echoed about the forest around me the hairs on the back of my neck literally stood straight up and I instinctively dropped to one knee in some sort of prehistoric hunter's defensive posture wondering what was about to run over me. In mere seconds my body was flooded with about a gallon and a half of adrenaline and my fight or flight mechanism came to full

alert. In that part of the state the cover is so dense that in the course of five days of hunting, I had no less than four similar up close and personal encounters with bulls screaming their heads off at me, yet I only saw one...the big guy in the first chapter of this book.

Bugling mature 6x6 bull   Photo - Vince Martinez

The typical mature elk bugle frequently consists of three parts though this is not always the case. The bugle begins with a low frequency raspy sound emanating from deep in the bull's gut that gradually rises to a high-pitched scream that can quickly carry across as many as three octaves often holding the highest note before promptly falling off quickly to another low frequency series of grunts or chuckles.

Here is a mental picture that some of us may remember that I hope will give you an idea of what I'm trying to describe. This is going to date me...so please keep the laughter to a minimum. Think of a bull's bugle as dropping the clutch (the bugle begins) on your 1969 three-speed Camero RS at a stoplight expecting to hear tires squealing and rubber burning only to discover to your chagrin that you have the car in 2nd gear and not 1st gear. What happens…all 350 horsepower is now trying its best to escape but the transmission will not let it. Slowly, yet in ever increasing increments (the bugle begins to shift into a higher frequency as more air is released) the Camero begins to move forward, faster and faster as the transmission catches up and releases all the energy that was trying to get loose. Now you shift into third gear (bugle octaves change) and the car zooms ahead achieving full release of the power within. The car is now at full bore (the peak of the bugle), then…with little warning all energy falls off, the engine gets quiet and then like an after thought it utters a few coughs…Uhug…Uhug…then silence again (the grunt and then the bugle ends). Remember…you're a sixteen-year-old kid and guess what…you're out of gas again!

A quick review of Physics 101 tells us that sound propagation is not as much a function of volume as it is of frequency. While volume (energy output) is a factor, it is the frequency of the sound that determines how far and through how much cover the sound can travel without distortion. High frequency sounds like those in the second part or scream of an elk bugle travel relatively short distances even though they are powered by a greater volume of air, while lower frequency sounds like those in the early stages of a bugle or the ending chuckle will actually carry for longer distances. Proof of this is evidenced by the US Navy's use of ELF or Extra Low Frequency sound for communication to its submarines that may be submerged and on patrol thousands of miles away from the source.

Bugling is first and foremost a means of advertisement to cows and bulls alike, and not as a challenge to fight to every bull in the valley, as many elk hunters believe. According to one of the most renowned elk researchers of all time, Valerius Geist, bulls bugle in an attempt to out advertise one another. It is the method bulls use to attract cows to them for the purpose of reproduction and when necessary to make their claim on the cows in their harem known to other interloper bulls that may be nosing around the periphery of the herd.

A dominance display by bugling bull   Photo - Vince Martinez

Bulls also bugle during the mating ritual. Since it is the cow who determines with which bull and when she will mate, bulls that make unwanted sexual advances to a cow that is not ready are often met with…well, rejection, i.e. the cow just walks off in a submissive posture. This rejection often causes the bull to emit a shortened version of its bugle, perhaps as some vocal signal of its frustration. On the flip side, when bulls successfully mount a cow that is ready to mate, the act is violently quick and typically ends with the bull jumping clear off the ground followed by a bugle. Go figure….

Urine Spraying

If much of the behavior elk exhibit during the rut is about advertisement, then I would be remiss if I failed to spend a few minutes talking about urine spraying. That's right, bull elk peeing all over themselves. No one ever said bull elk were much into personal hygiene and this definitely helps to make the argument. In reality urine spraying plays a vital role during the rutting ritual as another way that bulls advertise.

In late September of 2005, my wife, Rae Ann and I were attending Elk Fest in Estes Park, Colorado. Our work day had come to an end around 5:00 p.m. so we decided to take a tour around town to see if we could get some pictures of any of the hundreds of elk that can usually be found wandering through town during that time of the year. I know, this doesn't sound like much of a hunting story and it isn't, it's an elk behavior story and you observe elk behavior wherever the elk happen to be. This particular story took place on the Estes Park city golf course. Anyhow, back to the story. When we arrived at the golf course, we found about two hundred elk herded up into roughly four small groups grazing on some really nice Bermuda that made up one of the courses fairways. Each group was under the watchful eye of a dominant or herd bull, with anywhere from two to four satellite bulls drifting around the edge of each of the smaller groups presumably looking for an opportunity to sneak in and breed one of the cows.

The herd bulls were doing a first rate job running back and forth from one end of their respective harem to another chasing off raghorn after raghorn, all the while bugling at the top of their lungs to let the cows as well as the raghorns know who was in charge. Again clearly a form of advertisement as we saw no challenges to these brutes in the course of about two hours of observation. As we continued to watch one particular herd, I noticed that there was a nice 5x5 satellite bull that was starting to show some more aggressive behavior than the others. In one instance this particular bull decided that he had enough of these two-legged creatures (people) encroaching on what he must have considered his territory whereby he chased about three of those nearby over a fence. Actually it was pretty comical as one minute these tourists are snapping away with their digital cameras without a care in the world, even though some are within twenty yards of a pretty worked up bull and then all I could see was flip-flops and backsides flying over the fence. I thought I was going to split something I laughed so hard.

After running off the two-legged competition this bull must have been thinking pretty highly of himself as he began to spray. Spraying can take a number of forms from a light mist to a semi-directed stream, to a very heavy conical spray. The urine in most cases is directed at nearly right angles to the erected penis. Lowering his head almost to the ground the bull began in the semi-directed stream mode by spraying his face briefly then moving rearward to spray the heavy mane under his neck. He worked this area over for a good minute. All the while, the bull is palpitating. Palpitation is a rhythmic throbbing of the light colored area behind the penis and can be easily seen as it bobs during the spraying. Occasionally it would seem as if this particular bull would loose control of his aim as the urine stream would fire off to the left or right pretty much hosing down anything within four or five feet. Fortunately all the folks in colorful shorts and flip-flops were well out of range by now. Once the bull had exhausted what I thought must have been a gallon or more, the spraying ceased and the bull knelt down and began to rub and roll around in the overspray that had fallen on the ground…presumably to make sure that nothing went to waste. Actually, the urine soaked ground had muddied up pretty good and made for a fine yet small wallow. Often bulls will follow up this behavior by rubbing their recently soaked neck mane and the preorbital glands below their eyes on a nearby tree leaving some of the urine soaked mud that they picked up in the wallow as another form of territorial advertisement.

Herding and Harem Defense
The rut is a time of competition, collection, advertisement, and dominance. Cows seek out dominant bulls as a way of narrowing the field and assuring themselves that they have access to the best genetics for reproduction. Bulls are continually advertising to attract cows to themselves, conditioning the cows to remain nearby, and when necessary herding the cows to keep them from straying.

I recently observed two groups of cows each accompanied by a herd bull. Both groups were feeding on opposite sides of a small creek. If I had to estimate, I would guess that the groups were about two hundred yards apart yet the creek seemed to act as a physical barrier keeping the groups from mingling. For the better part of an hour the cows were content to remain in their respective groups. All the while each bull was on full time guard duty bugling and running from one end of his harem to another consoling his cows, keeping them nearby, and running off the younger satellite bulls that would from time to time attempt to make a run at one of the ladies. The bulls appeared to be equally matched in the five-year age range, one a nice 6x6 and the other a 6x7. Either of these bulls would have made a grand addition to any elk hunter's wall. Unfortunately, for me hunting season was already complete, and I was remanded to the sidelines with only a camera.

As I observed the two groups I wondered, what would happen if a few of these cows decided to cross the creek to the other bull? It was not long before I got my answer when a single cow dropped down into the creek and made her way over to the herd on the opposite side. I watched the two bulls to see what their respective reactions would be. While the gaining bull (bull #1) didn't seem to take much notice, the loosing bull (bull #2) that had been at the far end of the herd was getting pretty worked up. Regrettably for him there were two raghorns flirting around his end of the herd and he couldn't risk responding to the cow's departure with anything other than a parting "please come back sweetheart" bugle. I continued to watch the bull #1 on the opposite bank to see if there would be any sign of victory when I observed a second collared cow and her yearling calf start to make their way down into the creek about five minutes after the first. As she climbed the opposite bank, I guess her former boyfriend, bull #2, noticed her and this was about all he could take. Even though he appeared to be outweighed by the darker bull on the opposite side of the creek by at least a hundred pounds, bull #2 let out a husky roar and charged down the meadow about 75 yards and across the creek. I said to myself, this is going to be good as I waited for the battle to begin.

Bull #2 ran directly into the center of the cows on the opposite bank, stretched his neck and began to bugle and palpitate. Two things happened. The few cows that had scattered when he ran into the harem began to settle down and return to the group, and the larger darker bull #1 immediately trotted away about three hundred yards in complete submission. Clearly bull #2 even with lesser body size was able to make up the difference using a more assertive dominance display. Within ten minutes, with bull #1 now grazing farther down the meadow alone in defeat, the rest of bull #2s harem moved across the stream to join with the newly acquired harem to form a single group of about fifty cows.

Whenever one of the cows would begin to drift away, the new herd bull would lower his head below his shoulders and toss his antlers rearward along his back while moving towards the offending cow at an angle with his eyes averted often making a few grunts to console and encourage the cow to move back towards the herd. If the wayward cow failed to comply with this form of gentle persuasion, the bull would bring his antlers forward and make mock charges at the cow as a further enticement to get back in line. On a few occasions, I have actually witnessed bulls rush the cow and even horn them if their response was not want the bull wanted. Many times once the cow started to move back toward the herd, the bull would turn away from the cow and bugle. Since cows are really running the show, this bugle is more symbolic of the bull recognizing and acknowledging the cow's decision to submit and return to the herd.

Antlers fully erect posture   Photo – Jerry Gowins

Contrary to herding, bulls intent on mating with a particular cow will usually approach the cow from a more head on direction with his antlers fully erect. This communicates to the cow that his intent is other than merely herding. A cow that shows interest will allow the bull to move around behind her where he will begin licking her to determine if she has come into season yet. If the cow is not yet ready or decides that this bull is not the guy she wants to dance with after all, she will usually move away displaying a sign of submission. If she determines that the bull is 'the guy,' she will assume a rear leg spread haunch low posture. Many times you can actually see the cows rear legs begin to quiver as she prepares for the bull.

This brief discussion is offered to demonstrate that while herding prior to mating, the bull's attention is predominantly focused on acquiring and holding cows. The advantage to the hunter who is aware of this period of diverted attention should be clear. He should use this to his advantage by creating a plan to close for the shot, especially if bowhunting. It is critical to keep in mind however that while the bull's attention may be diverted, he is surrounded by perhaps dozens of sets of eyes (cows) that are continually looking for other prospective mates and predators as well.

The challenge is in not alerting the cows.   Photo - Jerry Gowins

Your challenge is to close to within effective shooting range without alerting the cows. Here you have to keep a keen eye on the wind. As cows are continually moving about the periphery of the herd, a smart hunter can use his cow call making soft comforting mews to cover unexpected footfalls as he moves in. If you pay close attention to the wind and use cover, you would be better to move in with no sound at all as any sound can attract attention regardless of how well you call. The less attention you can draw to yourself, the better off you will be. Keep in mind that when stalking bulls that are herding cows, your real challenge is to beat the cows' defense mechanism.

Elk Travel Patterns
As we discussed earlier, elk spend roughly ninety percent of their time, the exception being the rut, eating and resting. So how do they spend the remaining three to four hours of any twenty-four hour period? The areas in which elk feed throughout early to mid fall (hunting season) and the habitat in which they lay up during the day to digest can be separated by significant distances, often miles. The smart hunter who takes the time to study and understand how elk transition from one area to the other, and the factors that may play into why the elk use these specific routes stands a far greater chance at scoring on a high beamed bull or a fat cow, than the hunter who randomly traverses elk country taking his rifle or bow for an extended walk.

Keeping in mind our previous discussion on the Law of Least Effort, elk will use the same established trails year after year. Old travel routes usually found on timbered north or east facing slopes provide not only security but also make for ease of travel. For travel between drainages elk like to use saddles, often approaching them not straight on which requires a lot more effort, but by using existing trails that run nearly parallel but just below the ridge top so as not to highlight themselves. If the saddle is open or exposed, the elk may move left or right for cover soon after crossing the ridge. If there is open territory on the far side of the saddle with little cover, elk may pause or slow for a minute to make sure that the coast is clear before entering a meadow. If cover is available within the saddle itself, elk will almost always remain in the cover. In either case, placing a stand or setting up just over the saddle may give you an opportunity for a shot at a stationary or slow moving elk.

Elk have been known to use old stock trails in areas that are subject to summer grazing by cattle once the cattle have been moved out of the area to lower pasture. If you happen to come across a well-used stock trail, look closely for signs of elk usage as well. I can't tell you how many times I have missed elk sign because I failed to look for it. I had mentally written off the trail because I thought only cattle or sheep were using it.

Slopes
Though steep by human standards, slopes of ten to thirty percent are little challenge to elk for grazing or travel. I remember glassing a herd of elk in south central Colorado some years back on a scouting trip in late July. Though daytime temperatures were reaching into the seventies, there were still plenty of snow pockets trapped on northern slopes above 11,000 feet and these elk were scattered over a quarter-mile of this particular slope which in some places appeared to be as much as a forty percent grade. All the while they were feeding and staying cool lying in the snow as if they were on level ground. Research indicates that beyond about thirty percent, elk use usually drops off significantly, with little elk activity on slopes above fifty percent. However the same research shows that elk use tends to increase with an increase in slope with the highest frequency of use found on slopes in the fifteen to thirty percent range. Had we tried to make our way up the slope to the elevation where the elk were, I seriously believe our lungs would have burst. For the elk, it was just routine. The argument here is that just because the slope is tough on the hunter does not mean that you won't find elk there.

During early fall when temps may still spike into the high seventies, elk frequently use creek and drainage bottoms for travel routes because of the promise of water, high quality forage, and thermal cover from the heat of Indian summer days. Though difficult for the hunter to traverse because of the extreme density of cover found bordering such areas, hunters should not dismiss these travel routes. Look for stands where you can observe these corridors especially where they may open up near the heads of drainages. Also look for well used trails emerging from dark timber that feed into these creek bottoms. In areas where you can actually find moving water, look for elk sign in the cutbacks in the creek where water pools and elk may come to drink remaining under the cover of brush bordering the creek. While I am not a huge advocate of the use of tree stands for elk hunting, if you find an water source that is being frequented by elk, such would make for an excellent location to consider putting up a stand. See Chapter 9 for more on elk hunting from tree stands and blinds.

Learning About Land & Travel Patterns From the Air
Having spent an entire career strapped to the seat of fighter jet in the USAF/ANG, I have acquired a keen sense of the perspective one gains from looking over an area from altitude. While it is not for everyone, if you have the resources, it's really not that expensive, and you take the opportunity to spend even a small amount of time over flying the area that you plan to hunt, you will learn more about that area and the general travel patterns of elk in one hour than you will in a month of scouting on the ground. Don't get me wrong on this. I am not saying that flying over your hunting area is a replacement for quality time spent scouting on the ground. What I am saying is that the bird's eye view from the air will provide you with information and perspective that you will never get on the ground.

From the air, you will gain an acute sense of the typography of the land that perhaps 1% of hunters can discern from a topo map. If you have a topo of the area with you in the aircraft…even better as what you see will help to clarify what the map is telling you. Make sure to take your GPS along on the flight to mark spots that may be of interest once you actually get on the ground and begin hunting. In addition to learning how to access specific areas that you may want to hunt, the well used trails that elk leave in the open areas stand out clearly. In many cases you will see numerous trails paralleling one another across a slope indicating travel patterns. You will be able to see where these trails lead into dark timbered areas and where they come out on the opposite side. You will see which saddles are getting heavier use. Don't worry about seeing elk. That is not the objective. The over flight is to help you learn more about the area itself. If you do happen to see elk, well that's just icing on the cake.

Once the shooting begins elk tend to head to areas that are difficult for hunters to access. From the air, say 3,000-5,000 feet AGL (above the surrounding terrain) you will be able to look down into the bottom of some of those deep holes and cuts that you would in all likelihood never investigate, thus possibly missing out on a first-class elk area. If you plan to do some flying over elk country, make sure to check out the local laws in this regard. Depending upon the state that you plan to hunt, there may be regulations that limit the amount of time required between an over flight of an area and when you can actually begin hunting.

Because of the inherent difficulty of flying in mountainous terrain, it is critical that you never try to do this alone. Mountain flying in the Rockies is nothing like flying over flat farm land and many a wayward pilot has failed to come home because he headed his craft into the mountains with little or no mountain flying training. It's much safer to hire the plane and a competent mountain qualified pilot while you go along as the observer.

If you are planning on hunting Colorado or northern New Mexico and are looking for a first-class mountain qualified pilot (8000+ flight hours) and flight service, look to A-Cent Aviation located on the civil aviation side of the airport in Colorado Springs, Colorado. Mike and Alice Hogan along with their daughter Kim Skinner run A-Cent Aviation. In addition to one of the best flight schools in southern Colorado, they are also expanding flight services to offer a charter service that would be able to provide you with aircraft charter or rental. If you're interested, give A-Cent Aviation a call at (719) 573-2236 or check out their website at www.a-centaviation.com.

Chapter Four

Elk Hunting Is Not A Spectator Sport

To quote long time elk hunting authority and writer Jim Zumbo, "Elk hunting is the toughest, meanest, nastiest form of hunting in North America." Elk can inhabit some of the most challenging and even treacherous terrain found on the North American continent. On any given day in elk country the average hunter can expect to cover from as few as four to as many as twelve miles on foot, traversing all types of real estate ranging from miles of creek drainages covered with thick brush to dark timber blow downs that would test even the endurance of an Olympic athlete. Rocky talus covered slopes that limit the hunter's forward motion to two steps backward for every three steps forward are not uncommon. The amount of oxygen available to sustain the hunter above ten thousand feet is almost forty percent less than that available at sea level often causing a grown man to cry and ask for mercy or at least ask for a short break to catch his air. If that's not tough enough, consider that daytime temps can swing from the mid-teens or less before daybreak into the fifties, sixties, or even seventies during midday, then plummet just as rapidly as sunset nears back into subfreezing temps by nightfall. Nights in ElkCamp start out warm with full bellies, toasty sleeping bags, and woodstoves glowing cherry red, but by 2:00 am when nature calls, the fuel in the woodstove has usually run its course and the air in the tent has assumed a temperature very close to the temperature of the night air outside…cold…sometimes very cold.

Why do I paint what to many will seem like an incredibly unwelcoming and foreboding picture of elk hunting? Two reasons: to prepare the uninitiated pilgrim and to make a point, elk hunting can be and often is just plain hard, and it is without doubt not a spectator sport. To be successful at elk hunting requires a higher level of mental discipline than that required for most other types of North American hunting.

Maybe this tale from a past hunt will help clarify the point. One brisk October morning some years back, I set out from ElkCamp on foot just before 3:00 a.m. long before anyone else in the nearby camp had considered stirring from the warmth of their sleeping bags. This year I was hunting alone and my goal was to be on stand at the head of a drainage overlooking a small park where I expected elk would be feeding through most of the night before the elk began to move back towards their bedding area.

The little park was no more than a hundred feet across and perhaps a hundred and fifty feet long hidden on a slope in a stand of dark timber, but it provided the elk with two essentials, food and security. On one side was a small seep spring surrounded by a stand of bunch grass that had been burned by frost weeks earlier, but had since begun to cure making for a decent feeding ground for the elk in mid-October when sweet grasses can be few and far between. I expected the elk to begin filtering out of the park and up and over a saddle at the head of the drainage on their way to a recently used bedding area that I had discovered earlier. My thought was that they would start moving before daylight as the hunting pressure in the area was pretty heavy, which was about average for public land in Colorado. Once the pressure from hunters begins to affect the feeding patterns of the elk, they are rarely seen in the open during daylight hours as they begin their trek back to the security of their bedding areas in heavy timber long before the sun breaks. My hope was that the legal shooting hour would arrive before the elk would pass me on their way through the saddle above me, and I would be able to affect an ambush.

In order to make the climb to the drainage head I would have to ford a small stream that was perhaps eight feet across. It was too wide to jump across with a daypack and a rifle, so I had no choice but to walk across. I had crossed at a different point on the previous day so I wasn't sure how deep the water was beneath the thin layer of ice that had formed overnight. It was still pitch dark and I could hardly see where to step, but I knew I had to get a move on, so in I went. Thank goodness that my eight-inch waterproof boots were about two inches taller than the stream was deep at that point. Otherwise it would either have been a long cold wet hike, or I would have had to stop and dry my socks and boots, neither of which was appealing.

After two hours of climbing about fifteen hundred feet vertically in the space of about a mile and a half, I finally reached my stand about two hundred yards below the saddle at the top of the drainage. To say the least, after nearly three hours of hard humping from camp, which was based at almost 9,000 feet, I was whipped. Climbing up I had occasionally chirped on my cow call hoping that if I had made any noticeable noise, the elk that I figured were on the other side of the drainage would interpret it as just a wayward cow. As I took my stand between two Junipers, I looked up at the star-filled night sky. Only in elk country is the sky so awash with the brilliance of God's handiwork. During my climb up, the wind had cooperated and remained reasonably calm, but as soon as I sat down I detected that a slight breeze coming out of the north had picked up and was blowing from over the saddle down the slope past me. My mind said that this was not good as I figured the elk were still below me. I quickly looked for alternate stands but there were none. All I could do was hope that the elk were far enough offset across the drainage not to pick up my scent. Only time would tell.

As the first hints of silver and gray began to emerge in the eastern sky I started to detect the distant mews of cow elk conversing as they picked their way up the slope and out of the drainage. Determining distance through sound alone is nearly impossible, especially if you don't hear that well, so I wasn't sure when or where they might show themselves. It was the second rifle season in Colorado and I had an over-the-counter bull tag in a unit that had a four-point or better restriction. Hearing all those cows had me wishing I had put in for a cow tag, but it was too late to start second guessing myself now. Since that hunt so long ago, I have started hunting larger bulls, but for this hunt, I had my sights set on the first legal bull that showed.

After what I figured was about ten minutes I began to be able to see some movement on the opposite side of the small drainage from my perch. A quick glance through my binoculars confirmed that it was cow elk moving like silent ghosts weaving through the edge of the timber headed toward the saddle. Just minutes before they had been talking like they had no care in the world. Now there was only silence and moving shadows. With only one narrow shooting lane that was maybe ten yards across available to me, I continued to count cow after cow, but no bull appeared. In this area my experience had shown that most of the herds were small, usually numbering less than ten animals. By the time I counted ten cows, I was pretty sure that no bull was going to show. I had put my binocs down and was now watching the elk through my scope, hoping that should a bull show himself as the last in line pushing the cows, I would be ready to take the shot. I had just decided to put the rifle down and reconcile myself to being skunked, when I saw the glint of horns! I quickly glanced at my watch and sure enough, official sunrise had passed only a few minutes before, I was legal to take the shot. From just over a hundred yards, the shot would have been easy, but I couldn't get a good count on the number of points. The bull was filtering in and out of the brush just inside the edge of the timber. In my mind I could see all the horns I needed to see, but that just wasn't good enough. I visually tracked the bull for what seemed like two or three minutes, but could never get a good look at his rack that would confirm whether or not he was legal. I had been hunting hard for days and this bull was what I had worked for, what I had dreamed of for the 360 days since the last season's end. Surely he had a five-inch brow tine or four points on one side, the criteria for a legal bull in this unit. Alas, I wish I could tell you that this bull ended up in the freezer, but in the end I just could not make the call that he was legal and I had to pass on him.

I had put in day after day of hard hunting, rising many hours before dawn in freezing temps, enduring extensive lung-bursting humps up the mountain and in the end...the only choice I had was...no choice. I had to pass on the shot. Folks this is what I mean when I say that elk hunting is not a spectator sport. You have to get involved and go the whole distance resolved from the beginning that in the end things may not work out the way you want them to. Some days you win. Some days you lose.

In Elk Hunting 101 I talked about one's endurance being a key to successful elk hunting. Following up on that thought, let's briefly look at the mental and physical discipline that is an absolute if you want to be a successful elk hunter.

If you want to take the measure of whether or not you have the right stuff to become a successful elk hunter, ask yourself this one question, am I committed to doing whatever it takes? Simple huh? Not really. Sitting at home by a cozy fire or even in ElkCamp on the evening before your hunt begins, most of us will answer this question without hesitation in the affirmative. "Of course I have what it takes"…especially if there is another hunter around to hear your answer.

My encouragement here is not for the hunter who has for years consistently sacrificed, labored, endured horrible weather under the most undesirable of circumstances, but for those who have yet to accept the fact that such is the devotion of the true elk hunter. To repeat myself [from Elk Hunting 201] and to quote one of my personal heroes and one of the greatest American big game hunters of all time, President Teddy Roosevelt [inserts are mine]:

"The credit [success] belongs to the man in the arena [hunt] whose face is marred by dust and sweat and blood, who strives valiantly…who knows the great enthusiasms, the great devotions, who spends himself in a worthy cause, who at the best knows in the end the triumph of high achievement, and who at the worst, if he fails, fails while daring greatly, so that his place shall never be with those cold and timid souls who have known neither victory nor defeat."

I wish I could have said it as well. There is no place along the sidelines for the true and devoted hunter, for it is his devotion, his passion that will not permit it. He is compelled from within and from eons past to take up his spear, climb the mountain, and challenge the beast on his own ground.

Chapter Five

Locating Trophy Class Bulls

Before we start down this path, I think it would be practical to consider the question, what constitutes a trophy? According to Webster, the term trophy has its origins in the Latin referring to a memorial of an ancient Greek or Roman victory raised on the field of battle, or a representation of such a memorial inscribed on perhaps a medal; something gained or given in victory or conquest especially when preserved or mounted as a memorial. I especially like that last one…mounted as a memorial. So how big does a trophy have to be to make it to the wall? 260, 300, 360, 375, 400 or more. Over the years I have seen my share of wall hangers and to tell you the honest truth, there have been more of these trophies under the elusive 300-inches than over, but without exception, when the owner of the trophy shows it to you there is always a smile on their face and a true sense of accomplishment in their eyes. Perhaps the old saying is true; beauty is in the eye of the beholder. Let's take a look at what some notables in the industry have to say about what constitutes a record buck bull.

Locating a 300+ bull can be a challenge.   Photo - Vince Martinez

The Boone and Crockett Club

Known for it's strict adherence to a Fair Chase doctrine, the Boone and Crockett Club has, since its founding in 1887 by Theodore Roosevelt, been recognized as a leader in issues that affect hunting, wildlife and wild habitat. The Boone and Crockett Club promotes selective hunting for mature big game species as a game management tool for maintaining balanced and healthy herd populations. The Club's North American Big Game records program serves as a vital conservation record for documenting the success of wildlife management programs.

The scoring system depends upon carefully taken measurements of the enduring trophy characteristics to arrive at a numerical final score that provides instant ranking for all trophies of a category. By measuring only enduring characters (such as antlers, horns, and skulls) rather than skin length or carcass weight, the measurements may be repeated at any later date to verify both the measurements and the resulting ranking in each category. The system places heavy emphasis on symmetry, penalizing those portions of the measured material that are non-symmetrical. This results in even, well-matched trophies scoring better and placing higher in the rankings than equally developed but mismatched trophies, a result that most people readily agree with and accept. For those antlered trophies with unusual amounts of abnormal antler material, non-typical categories were developed to give them recognition, as they would be unduly penalized in the typical categories. Trophies that meet the Awards minimum but not the All-Time minimum will be listed in the Awards book. Trophies that meet the All-Time minimum will be listed in both the Awards book, as well as "Records of North American Big Game."[1]

Minimum Entry Scores:

	Awards	All-Time
American Typical Elk	360	375
American Non-Typical Elk	385	385
Tule Elk	270	285
Roosevelt's Elk	275	290

Pope and Young Club
Founded in 1961 and modeled after the Boone and Crockett Club, the Club advocates and encourages responsible bowhunting by promoting quality, fair chase hunting, and sound conservation practices. Via its Records Program, the Pope and Young Club encourages excellence in bowhunting by arousing awareness and promoting exceptional examples

of American big game. The Club records information on North American big game taken with bow and arrow.[2]

Minimum Entry Scores:

American Typical Elk	260
American Non-Typical Elk	335
Roosevelt's Elk	225

Safari Club International
Safari Club International Foundation (SCIF) is a 501(c)(3) charitable organization that funds and manages worldwide programs dedicated to wildlife conservation, outdoor education and humanitarian services. SCI provides value to its members by shaping policies and legislation that protect the freedom to hunt.[3]

Minimum Entry Scores:

	Min. General	Min. Archery
Rocky Mtn. Typical Elk	265	235
Rocky Mtn. Non-Typical Elk	278	247
Roosevelt's Elk	245	220
Tule Elk	245	220

For the purposes of this discussion I am going to use 300 B&C as a baseline when referring to trophy bulls. In over ten years of working with clients looking for a trophy elk hunt, better than the 300-point threshold is what most indicate they are talking about when asked to define what the word trophy means to them. Every western elk state holds a share of these 300-class or better bulls, some far more than others but for most hunters the big question is how do we plan a hunt for a trophy bull? By the way, if you were hoping that we would tell you exactly where to find a trophy bull that is not going to happen here. What we are going to do is give you some good tips that will help you get your homework moving in the right direction. Those who take the time to invest themselves in the preparation, more often than not reap rewards that are far greater than those who don't take the time.

Search the Record Books

If you are really looking for an area that will produce a bull that will get you in the books, go directly to the source. All three of the above mentioned organizations track the information on where bulls entered into their record book were taken. Usually the entry will have a reference to a city, town, or county in the particular state where it was taken. It will also usually indicate the year (if available) in which the animal was harvested. A few hours of research will start to give you a picture of which states and which areas within that state produce the bigger bulls.

Outfitters Association's Best of Species Awards

Some states have Outfitter Associations that track trophy harvests of their member outfitters. Each year the association awards something similar to a "Best of Species" award to the outfitter who brings in the biggest bull. In many states you will see the name of the same outfitter popping up year after year. It is then just a matter of finding out which area(s) that outfitter hunts to narrow down your search for an area that produces bigger or trophy class bulls. If the outfitter hunts on the National Forest or BLM land, the US Forest Service or BLM maintains this information respectively.

State By State

Arizona: If you're looking to set a new world record, Arizona offers some of the best opportunities for 400-class or better bulls and the South Kaibab may be at the top of the list. While drawing one of the coveted tags in this area with low hunting pressure and strong genetics is extraordinary, it is not impossible. Some of the best public land opportunities for trophy bulls can be found in units 9 and 10. Other areas producing B&C bulls include units: 4A, 5A&B, 6A&B, 7 and 8. For those who can afford the price tag, the San Carlos Apache reservation may offer the best genetics in the state. If you are not in a position to pay big bucks, look closely at the public land surrounding the reservation.

New Mexico: 320 to 330-class bulls can be found regularly in Units 16A-E, 21A and 21B of New Mexico's Gila National Forest, and bulls exceeding 350 are not all that uncommon for the hunter who is willing to put some miles on his boots in this Pinon-Juniper covered wilderness. Other areas with good trophy potential include units 4, 10, 12, 13 and 55. For those able to afford the price of admission, The Mescalero Apache Reservation usually produces at least one 400-class monster each year. A more affordable hunt can usually be found on the Jicarilla Apache Reservation, but while you will likely see 350 or better bulls, you probably won't encounter anything approaching the 400-class bulls found on the Mescalero Apache Reservation. Keep in mind that all elk tags (except land owner tags) in New Mexico are obtained via a lottery and it may take years of applying before you draw. The strategy for hunting states that only offer tags via a draw system is to begin putting in for as many of these states as you can and have a backup plan for hunting one of the states offering over-the-counter tags such as Colorado or Idaho until you draw.

Utah: If you're planning on hunting one of Utah's premium limited-entry areas be prepared to part with some cash. 2006 non-resident tags run $1500. Though not a state typically know for record elk harvests, Utah has produced most of the biggest bulls in recent years. Areas to consider if your planning a big bull hunt in Utah include: Book Cliffs, North Slope-Three Corners, North Slope-Summit and West Daggett, Box Elder-Grouse Creek and Box Elder-Pilot Mountain.

ELK HUNTING 301…Making It Happen In Elk Country

Colorado: While Colorado hosts the largest elk herd anywhere numbering in excess of 300,000 (2006) and is known as the elk hunting capital of the world for turning out the largest elk harvest annually, it is not necessarily known for delivering large numbers of trophy class bulls as compared to other states. This does not, however, mean that Colorado does not produce a respectable share of 300-class or better bulls each year. For the public land hunter GMU 76 offers excellent opportunities for larger bulls. Just west of Montrose GMU 62 is also another favorite. GMU's 86 and 861 in the southern Sangre de Cristos are another destination for those seeking trophy class bulls, but be prepared to pay to hunt private land or do a backpack type hunt as the access to public land is limited and the terrain can be brutal. Farther north GMU 14 in the Mt. Zirkel Wilderness usually produces some really nice bulls as well. Keep in mind that hunting areas designated as wilderness means you will be limited to foot or horseback travel as there are no motorized vehicles allowed in these areas. Also look to the Gore Range at the higher elevations. Lower elevations on public land are heavily hunted forcing more mature bulls to hide out as high as they can get.

One of the best-kept secrets for bigger bulls in Colorado is private ranches (fair chase hunting) that consistently hold trophy 320 to 385-class bulls and are located east of I-25 in the southern Colorado Pinyon-Juniper mesas. To look at these ranches you would never guess that they hold elk, but as someone once said, "Looks can be deceiving." While these are few and far between, for prices not too far above those of public land guided hunts, a smart hunter has an excellent chance of scoring on the bull of a lifetime. One particular ranch that I know of boasts a bull to cow ratio of 100:100 and will not allow hunters to take bulls less than 320 B&C. If you are interested in looking into one of these hunts, contact ElkCamp.com Outdoor Adventures us via our website, www.ElkCamp.com.

Nevada: If you are lucky enough to draw a tag, Nevada offers some of the best opportunities for coming home with a huge trophy bull. For example, in 2004 almost 70% of the bulls taken carried 6-point or better racks. If you want to focus on really large Nevada bulls look to units 111-115 around Ely. The genetics throughout Nevada are good, but those found around Ely are truly exceptional.

Wyoming: If you're looking for bigger bulls in Wyoming a number of destinations come to mind, first is the area surrounding the National Elk Refuge in Jackson Hole. While hunting on the refuge is not allowed, there are a number of migration routes leading to it where a strategically placed hunter might do well, particularly in the Gros Ventre range. One also might want to consider east of Yellowstone National Park.

Montana: Areas around Yellowstone and Glacier National Parks and along the Idaho-Montana border produce some extremely nice bulls. Due to the ruggedness of this terrain hunting pressure is relatively light. If you like straight up and straight down, this is the area for you. Bulls on both sides of the border seem to achieve the desired 6x6 racks somewhat earlier than bulls in the eastern part of the state.

Idaho: For whatever reason, Idaho seems to have remained a well-kept secret as a haven for bigger bulls. This may be due to the difficulty in navigating the terrain in much of the state. If there is one word to describe elk hunting in Idaho it is…tough. Few are those who are willing to make the effort required to get on these big Idaho bulls. Areas to consider include: the Salmon River drainage, Teton, Kootenai, Shoshone, and Fremont counties. In addition to Colorado it is also one of the few remaining states where over-the-counter tags are still available (2006).

ELK HUNTING 301...Making It Happen In Elk Country

Trophies like this require commitment.   Photo - Jerry Gowins

If your looking to hook up with a trophy class bull on public land, you need to be mentally and physically prepared to do whatever it takes and go wherever you have to in order to find them. You need to get smart on why elk do what they do. For the average elk hunter looking to score on any legal bull, 80% of the effort will be in finding the elk. When you narrow your search down to that small group of bulls that have survived at least five hunting seasons and likely six, seven or even eight seasons, now locating that bull becomes about 98% of your effort. Luck notwithstanding; there is little chance of bumping into a 300-class or better bull anywhere near areas that are frequented by other hunters. Drainage heads with succulent grasses, moist valley floors, timbered transition areas, the bottom of the ugliest hole you can find, these are places to start looking. If you are considering a stand, ask yourself, does it overlook a well used food or water source, does it offer security, is it on or near a transition route, is it far...far away from other hunters, is there an elk standing in the middle of it? If yes is not the answer to at least one of the above, consider another location.

Chapter Six

A Veteran Elk Hunter's Thoughts On Success

Thought #1…If your plan is to have a great time in elk country and should you bag an elk, then that is just icing on the cake…you are my kind of hunter and will in all probability have a first-class adventure that you will want to share with friends and family for years to come.

Thought #2…If you're hunting public land that you are not familiar with and plan on holding out for a huge bull because you drove 1,000+ miles and spent $1,500 on gear and licenses…plan on being disappointed.

Thought #3…**P**rior **P**lanning **P**revents **P**oor **P**erformance

Thought #4…A cheap cow call or bugle in the hands of someone who knows how and when to use it can be the key to his success.

Thought #5…An expensive cow call or bugle in the hands of a fool who doesn't know that he doesn't know what he is doing will be his own undoing.

Thought #6…All the gear in the world will not make up for a shortfall in planning, experience, commitment, or sound judgment.

Thought #7…Listen more, speak less, help a friend in need, and be willing and able to hump uphill and down forever.

Thought #8…All the scent cover-up products in the world will not cover-up bad personal hygiene and sittin' in the cook tent in your huntin' duds. Scent kills. If you are using scent management systems, don't forget that guys sweat a lot around the neck and head (hatband). These are areas that are usually not covered by these systems. Carry some unscented wipes and a Ziploc bag to store them in.

Thought #9…The kill zone on a mature bull elk is approximately eighteen inches in diameter. Does that mean that if your shot group at the range is consistently inside that circle that you are well prepared? No, because that kill zone is predicated on a perfect broadside shot at a known range on a non-maneuvering elk that is cooperating. What happens when your target is moving or quartering towards or away from you? The aspect of the kill zone will change. That eighteen-inch circle may now only be six inches. Your target is a small two-inch cylinder passing at a minimum through the heart or both lungs. See only the cylinder.

ELK HUNTING 301...Making It Happen In Elk Country

Thought #10...Outside of the rut, and sometimes during the rut, it is the cow that is calling the shots in an elk herd, not the bull. To bag the bull you have to beat the cows first.

Thought #11...They are antlers...not horns.

Thought #12...Bull elk bugle as a form of male advertisement not as a challenge to a fight. When bulls bugle back and forth during the rut it is typically one bull trying to advertise his superiority over that of the other bull. The exception to this is that bulls tend to bugle when a cow that is not ready or willing to breed with that bull spurns their sexual advance.

Thought #13...While the volume or sound of a bull's bugle may be an indicator of its age, this is not always an infallible indicator. I've watched old herd bulls with large harems that on their best day could only manage a raspy cough.

Thought #14...Burns can provide elk with new growth that is up to fifty percent more nutritious than the food was before the burn for up to three years following the fire. Small burns are good places to look for bulls. Cows typically avoid smaller burns because they do not allow the cow to see enough area to set her self-protection mechanism at ease.

Thought #15...I believe that the most important characteristic when choosing a reliable elk cartridge is to choose the largest North American big game cartridge that you can shoot well and consistently. 30-06, 7MM Remington Mag, .300 WSM, .300 Winchester Mag, .300 Remington Ultra Mag, .338 Mag are all excellent choices for elk. Bullets like the Nosler Partition, Winchester FailSafe, and Swift Scirocco are exceptional choices for penetration on elk at long ranges.

Thought #16...Stay put just a little longer. This is a tough one for me personally, but the results speak for themselves.

Those who stay on stand longer usually come home with more elk.

Wolf Pack Systems camo helps Kevin Fair disappear while glassing.

Thought #17...Those who spend the most time looking for elk seem to be the ones doing most of the finding. Spend as much time as possible on high vantage points glassing with a good spotting scope and tripod. Focus on fringe areas, small parks within heavily wooded areas, saddles, and water sources. This is not the time to get in a hurry. Locating elk from a distance and then planning a stalk is much easier than chasing them down after you stumble over them. A good lightweight tripod will allow you to glass longer as it will do all the work of supporting the scope.

Thought #18...When hunting high pressured elk, try to discover when the hunters in other camps in the area are heading out in the morning, then plan on leaving camp at least an hour earlier to get farther up the mountain. The hunters arriving on the mountain later will act as a driving force on elk down low for you.

Thought #19…Take along a large contractor bag with a small amount of dirt in the bottom (some use apples). When you come in from hunting at the end of the day, strip off your hunting duds and drop them in the bag immediately. Then tie off the bag until the next morning. This will help to keep camp odors from permeating your hunting clothes and add an earthy cover scent to your gear.

Thought #20…If you come across an area where elk have bedded, look carefully at the tracks leading out of the bedding area. Elk that left in a hurry will leave sets of tracks widely spaced because they jumped up and bounded away, whereas elk that did not leave in a hurry will usually leave evenly spaced tracks. Also look for urine spots as elk often urinate in their beds upon standing. Cows will leave a urine spot near the fringe of the bed's indentation, bulls pee right in the middle of their bed.

Thought #21…Following the rut and before deep snows move into the high country, look for big bulls up higher. A general rule of thumb is…the higher the bigger. The reason for this is that mature bulls are very solitary following the rut and will seek out secluded areas where they can recover, feed, and be left alone. Younger bulls are often found lower down the mountain and may even be found on the fringe of a herd of cows.

Thought #22…If an extreme cold snap moves through while you are in camp, start looking for increased elk movement. Elk require more food to stay warm during these conditions. If the cold is accompanied by snow it may force the elk to shift their feed and bedding areas thus becoming more visible as they move about.

Thought #23…When elk bed down during the middle of the day, they will get up every few hours and may move as much as ¾ of a mile as they feed before returning to their bedding area. This can make midday an excellent time to catch elk in fringe areas.

Chapter Seven

A Serious Bowhunter's Secrets to Success

Lew Claspell

I have been hunting in Colorado for the last twenty-eight years, starting at the tender age of 14. This at the time was the minimum age for a youth to start big game hunting in this state. I hope to share some secrets that will guide any bowhunter to success in hunting elk. These secrets can also be incorporated into the rifle hunter's handbag of tricks.

In the early years of my first decade of elk hunting with a rifle, Colorado didn't have a point restriction. The bulls were scarce and it was not uncommon to see spike bulls that were herd bulls. Colorado then imposed a 4-point restriction on bulls, meaning that a bull had to have at least 4-points or better to be harvested, and within a few years, branch-antlered bulls became pretty common. About the same time, Colorado began acquiring a reputation as an excellent state in which to pursue big game such as mule deer and elk. Tags are readily available over the counter, and there were vast sections of public land for hunters to take advantage of. Due to the ever-increasing number of hunters we were encountering, my brother Bill and I decided we no longer wished to participate in the rifle seasons so we took up hunting with the bow to escape the crowds and to enable us to hunt the rut and bugling bulls!

The first couple of years we stumbled around the forest learning from mistakes and missed opportunities. During the first year out, I can clearly recall the two big 6x6 bulls that I missed at close range. I can also remember another big 6x6 bull that I never drew on because my confidence had been diminished. Hopefully those who are reading this will take it to heart and learn from my mistakes, thus reducing the learning curve and leading them to success.

After the season closed on our first year of hunting with archery equipment, we both agreed that we were hooked. We began our planning right after the close of the season for the next year, and by doing so we were more successful the following season. Here's how we did it.

Pick a Spot
Most Bowhunters have heard this before, but it is not what you may think. By "pick a spot," I mean, picking a spot to focus your hunting efforts in. As a rule, picking a GMU

ELK HUNTING 301…Making It Happen In Elk Country

(Game Management Unit) is not as simple as looking at the brochure and saying I think we'll go to unit X.

There should be a good deal of homework and research that goes into picking your hunting spot(s). There are several good resources available to help you choose a location where you can reasonably expect to at least be in the same general area as a herd of elk. The Colorado Division of Wildlife posts a link to the hunting recaps for the previous years on their website, http://wildlife.state.co.us/. These summaries contain a wealth of valuable information: elk harvest broken into cow vs. bull, number of hunters in the unit, also for those looking to hunt in limited areas, the number of licenses available and how many preference points are required to draw a tag. When you have located an area that you think has some potential, highlight it with a yellow highlighter. After you have several GMUs picked out, you can move on to the next step.

The next step should be to call the area biologist with the Colorado Division Of Wildlife (CDOW). Have a list of questions written out before hand to ask. Remember these folks are often located in a busy office and may not have a lot of time to spend with you. Keep your questions short and to the point.

Questions you will want to ask:
1. What is the number of elk in GMU (#?) before and after hunting season?
2. Did the area have a winterkill? How much (percentage)?
3. What is the hunting pressure?
4. What is the average age of bulls in the area?
5. What is the bull to cow ratio? (bulls per 100 cows)
6. What is the hunter success rate? (which is also on the hunt recap).

You can add your own questions to this list, but make sure to have them written down before you call. Finally, remember to thank them for their time. Did the answers to your questions satisfy your curiosity? If not ask about the other areas you have selected.

Once you have settled on a GMU that has potential, there are several other things that you can do to put the ball in your court. Contact the USFS for the forest the GMU is located in. Ask them about planned burns, camping locations, how much usage is the land seeing for other recreational activities, such as fishing, hiking, off-road (ATV usage). I try to avoid areas where there is a high summer usage.

Does the area that you selected still sound favorable? If so, it's time to start looking at maps. There are many on-line map sources that can be used from the comfort of your home, or if you can get by with it, at your office, like those found on www.elkcamp.com. Look for water sources, small parks, and benches on the North slopes. Also check for Forest Service roads to access these areas or at least get close to them. It is not unusual to walk a mile or more into the best area of a given location. Most of the on-line maps will also give you GPS coordinates, write these down if you can use them in your GPS. If you have computer mapping software such as Maptech®, Delorme®, or one of the many GPS manufacturers mapping programs, by all means use these. Once you have a pretty good idea of what the lay of the land is like, use the on-line satellite maps, such as Teraserver®. These will show you very good detail on the type of vegetation that is in the area.

I like to use my mapping software and plot routes and waypoints, which can be uploaded to the GPS unit that I carry. Some of the better mapping software can show you public vs. private land. I have located several honey holes, by using this feature to find where public land kisses private land. There may only be about 100 yards or less, but it can open up to many thousands of acres that are other wise land locked by private land.

Now you have a GMU where you know the health of the elk herd, and a general knowledge of the land. You should have ordered a good map of the whole area too, which you can have laminated to protect it against the elements. But you really don't know what you are going into yet unless you have been out there before.

That leads us to scouting the area during the late summer if possible. For most folks who do not live in elk country, that may be impractical. But there is always the chance the family vacation can be taken in the Rockies. Most families enjoy coming out, as there are things for everyone in the family to enjoy. Don't expect to haul your family into the woods and live in a tent for a week or more. Instead stay close to a town where there are things that they may be able to participate in. Plan day trips into your hunting area leaving as early as you can for a better chance at seeing game. During these summer scouting excursions I look for cows and calves. Knowing that if I can keep tabs on the cows during the summer, the bulls will join them in September. If you are fortunate enough to be able to come out before the season, spend a little time at the local café. Especially look for the ones that have a lot of pickup trucks parked out front. Sit as close as possible to any rancher types that may be in there and try to start a conversation with them. Buying a couple of cups of coffee can go a long way. Tell them what you are doing in the area. Most of the locals in the small mountain towns hunt; they may not tell you the location of their honey hole, but you can gather a bunch of information from them, once they start talking to you.

During the scouting trip(s), look for old rubs located on the lodge pole pines. These areas are spots the bulls will return to year after year. Also check water sources, these should be marked on your GPS. Seeing elk is always a bonus! Expect to see game early and late in the day during the summer months. Taking the family on a drive in the forest is a good way for everyone to try and spot game.

You should try and locate a couple of places that may be a place for your hunting camp. Where I hunt, we have used the same camping spot for over 14 years now. Others who frequently hunt there know we camp in that spot and leave it for us. But keep in mind there may be someone else camped out there when you arrive, so always have a couple of backup spots.

There is only so much you can expect to see and do during a family outing. Keep this in mind, and don't let it bother you if you do not see any elk during this trip. But you should at least find tracks and sign that elk are living in this area. If not, you will need to venture into another location until you have found these signs. Once you have found sign that there are indeed elk living in the area, focus your attentions on this and the area within about five square miles of where you find the most sign. This is where you will start your hunt in September.

Get Into Shape
Elk can live in some of the roughest terrain in the state of Colorado, often on steep mountain hillsides at elevations over 12,000 feet. They can also be in a particular drainage on Monday and be in the next zip code on Tuesday. A hunter planning on doing a do-it-yourself (DIY) style hunt must be in the best physical condition they can possibly be in before heading out. It is very easy for me to put on 10 pounds of unwanted weight during the winter months, mostly between Thanksgiving and Christmas. During January, I start my initial workout for elk hunting. This workout includes 30 minutes 4-

6 times a week on an elliptical trainer. Any workout designed for hunting should include a good cardio program.

Do whatever you can to build up your stamina: running, walking, bicycling. But first consult your physician and discuss your plans for the upcoming hunt. Have a full physical done; everyone should do this at least once a year. There are many books written on this subject so I will not dwell on it. I just want to make a reference to it, since being in the best physical shape will allow you to have a more enjoyable hunt.

Perfect Practice
Being an avid archer who truly enjoys shooting a bow, I am tuned-up year round. I like to practice from twenty to sixty yards on the target range that my boys and I frequent. Now I know there are many out there who will blast me for longer yardages, to which I reply: Elk are big creatures, two times the size of a deer. Most will not hesitate to take a 30-yard shot on a whitetail buck. With the size difference, a 60-yard shot is very achievable with modern compound bows. However, I do believe in pinpoint accuracy, and will pass on any shot that is questionable.

My practice sessions contain a good deal of shooting from a kneeling position. Of the fifteen elk I have taken with a bow, only two were shots that were made from a standing position. I enjoy shooting unmarked 3-D ranges, and twice a week from the spring until fall finds me on the local range after work and on Saturday mornings getting in a couple of rounds of shot placement and yardage estimation. During these shoots, I wear my hunting gear, including a daypack.

The first season that I missed the two big 6x6 bulls, I had only practiced from a standing position at known yardage. The first bull was broadside at 45 yards, I missed him low thinking he was closer to 35 yards. The second bull was close enough to spit on, I shot over his back. By failing to practice yardage 'guesstimation', I had committed the cardinal sin of the bowhunter. During my elk hunting setups, if time permits I use a laser rangefinder quickly ranging trees or rocks on the path I expect the bull to come in on. This helps take some of the guesswork out of making a clean and ethical shot.

Practice sessions should include drawing your bow smoothly; coming to anchor, acquiring the target, and a clean release with follow through. Practice only until your groups start to widen, then put your gear away for the next day. Fatigue will lead to bad habits in a hurry, which will be magnified when you are shooting broadheads at live game.

A person who is new to archery can benefit from a coaching session at the local pro shop. With just a few months of practice with today's modern compound bows; a beginning archer can become proficient enough to go elk hunting. It takes a good deal of dedication to become an expert shot with archery tackle. Unlike shooting a rifle, one must continue to shoot year round to keep the muscles tuned up. But most archers will tell you; it's fun to shoot their bows.

Calling All Elk
Elk are very social and vocal animals. They will call to each other when moving from the bedding area to the feeding areas and vise versa.

Get a couple of DVDs or CDs on elk calling and practice on the drive to work and home. Your spouse will appreciate this! Learn the different sounds of elk talk, and try a variety of calls to find the ones that you can use with ease. I like to use mouth diaphragm calls, specifically the pallet plate call. I also carry a bugle. The bugle is used to locate the bulls. Then I use a mixture of cow, calf, and satellite bugles or spike squeals to try and draw a bull in closer for a shot. If there is an elk farm close by, you can listen to the sounds of real elk, and see how they respond to your calls.

Hunting Techniques That Work

In order to be successful on elk, you must hunt them where they live. Elk can often travel many miles in a single day looking for food, water, shelter, or companionship.

After arriving at your chosen location, and setting up camp, you are prepared for the opening day of elk season. The opener finds you hiking into a bowl brimming with anticipation and enthusiasm a mile or more from the nearest road, where you spotted some elk earlier in the year. Daybreak however, finds you on top of a mountain without any elk in sight, and not a single bugle to be heard. What happened to the elk?

This scenario is repeated year after year. You must consider where the elk were and why did they leave. Chances are the elk are close to this area, something changed and they moved for a more favorable location. Either the water source has changed or they have found a better food source. Unless they were spooked out of this area they should be within a mile or two from where they were when you spotted them in the late summer. This is where the hours of cardio are going to pay off. You must hike the ridge tops, glassing and calling into different drainages until you have again located the animals. Once you have them located, you can hunt, and possibly harvest one. Here's how I go about it.

Locating Elk

If the elk are no longer in the last place I saw them, I will determine if they moved for a better location due to water or food. Then I will consult my maps for water sources. Water is one of the best things you can find here in the arid parts of the west. Along with a good water supply will be good grass for the elk to feed on. I will scout these areas during the afternoon lulls, from about 12:30 pm until 3:00 pm, looking for evidence that the elk have relocated into these areas. Once I have found fresh sign, I will formulate a game plan, based on the new location.

If it is real dry, as it has been during the past five years (now 2006), due to drought conditions it may be best to stay close to the water source. If the elk are undisturbed they will not travel far from water, usually remaining within a mile of it. The last thing you want to do is to bust these elk in their bedding areas inadvertently. If you do, they may not return for several days. Instead, stake out an area between the bedding area and the water. Once you have found the bedding area, you can often call a bull out by setting up five hundred yards away, and calling like a lost cow. If I have a herd located I will only hunt them in the morning and late afternoon.

During the middle of the day, I return to camp and shower, practice with my bow, eat lunch, then go out and scout for other herds. The herd I have located is not going anywhere as long as I do not spook them from their beds. This gives me time to locate another herd or two. Good hunting.

Chapter Eight

Hunting With A Professional Outfitter… If There Is A Short Cut This May Be It

There is nowhere you will learn more about elk hunting faster than on a fully guided hunt with a reputable professional outfitter. A good outfitter is in the business of elk hunting or planning for elk hunts 365 days per year. They live elk hunting, breathe elk hunting, and sleep elk hunting. It's not a hobby or a desire to hunt with their buddies that drives professional outfitters. It is how they make a living, and if they do not consistently produce quality hunts for their clients, they do not stay in business for long. Licensed professional outfitters are at the top of their game. For the elk hunter who is either new to the sport or does not have the time necessary to devote to learning how elk live and move in a particular area in preparation for an upcoming hunt, an outfitter may be your best resource for success.

Statistics tell us that the average elk hunter is successful one year out of every eight. Such data can reflect a wide range of variables including: adverse weather, drought, herd dispersion, predation, food supply, hunting pressure, a hunter's stamina, and more. The one factor that may have more effect on success than any other however, is a hunter's preparation and participation…or lack thereof.

Every year via ElkCamp.com Outdoor Adventures, I am contacted by thousands of hunters looking for the best opportunity they can find for a successful elk hunt. While I haven't actually tracked the exact statistics of these contacts, I can reasonably estimate, in the eleven years that I have been a hunting consultant, 60% of those contacts are from hunters who whole-heartedly expect to spend a week in elk camp and go home with a cooler full of elk steaks, yet they have either never been elk hunting, or they have absolutely no idea where or maybe even how to hunt elk. Folks, in my opinion this is about the same as giving your 12-year-old child the keys to the family car and sending him off across town to run an errand. The chance of him coming home with the goods, the car in one piece, and absent any form of bodily injury is remote. He doesn't know how to drive, doesn't have the first clue about how to navigate the terrain, and as a result runs a pretty good chance of injuring himself and others. Why would you consider doing such as thing? Well of course you would never consider doing that. So why do so many would-be elk hunters head out into elk country every year unprepared and lacking the required knowledge and ability to achieve a safe and successful hunt? In short and in most cases it comes down to two things, a perceived lack of money to fund a guided hunt and too much ego causing the average hunter to think that he knows more about elk hunting than he actually does. Let's look at an example that I believe will

ELK HUNTING 301...Making It Happen In Elk Country

help you see the value of hunting at least once with a quality professional outfitter.

To make sure that we are comparing apples to apples we need to compare the actual costs required of the hunter to achieve the same level of success with an outfitter as hunting on his own. For purpose of this argument, I will set this at a 65% probability of success. In short what does it take or cost for a hunter to achieve a 65% probability of success?

Cost of an Average Successful Outfitter Hunt
The average cost of a fully-guided elk hunt in Colorado, the most popular elk hunting destination on the planet is about $3,500 plus the cost of tags and travel, so let's round that up to $4,500. Granted some guided hunts cost more, but this is the average for 2006. In return for your investment here is what the hunter can reasonably expect.

- Opportunity success ratio typically in excess of 50%. Many outfitters can demonstrate consistent annual average ratios in the 75-80% opportunity range. Opportunity is the true measure of the abilities of the outfitter. This measures the ability of the outfitter to place a hunter in the position to have a reasonable opportunity to take a shot at a legal animal. Unlike a true success ratio (above), the kill ratio also includes a metric for the hunter missing the shot or passing up the shot for a chance at a better animal. Kill ratios are not true measures of the outfitter's ability but include the actions and abilities of the hunter as well.
- An experienced elk hunting guide who is intimately familiar with the area to be hunted, understands elk habits and behavior, knows their travel and feeding habits in the area, has knowledge of the use of calls, and knows how to place his client in the position to have a shot at a legal animal. Value: $200 per day x 5 days = $1,000.

- A ready made camp complete with cook, heated sleeping tents or cabins with padded cots, a warm comfy cooking and eating tent, three nourishing meals every day (plus almost all the midday snacks you can eat), hot coffee and hot water available at almost anytime, plenty of clean safe drinking water that you don't have to haul, all cooking and dishwashing is provided by staff, and a covered facility for taking care of personal business (sometimes heated and stocked with hunting magazines). Value: $950.
- Daily hunting transportation usually in the form of rider friendly mountain ready riding and packhorses or mules. Value: $350.
- Wrangler: this is the guy or gal who gets up two hours before your alarm goes off in the wee hours to feed, water and prepare your mount (horse) for the day's hunt. He is also the one to whom you hand off your horse at the end of the day to feed, water, unsaddle, and care for. (Another hour). Oh...and if the horse gets loose and runs off a few miles, gets sick or goes lame, this is the guy who takes care of those problems as well. Value: $300 (and this is a steal).
- Packers who weigh, load and haul all of your personal gear up and down the mountain so you don't have to, and field dress your elk and pack it from the kill site all the way down the mountain to your truck. Value: $200. (This is another steal!)
- A professional licensed insured outfitter who in most cases will handle all of the planning and licensing application process for you. Who will be there to take care of your every need 24 hours a day and will attend to your needs should you become sick or injured. Value: you decide
- Cost to the outfitter for permits, advertising, insurance. Value: $200

- Profit to the outfitter after expenses: $500.
- Tags. Cost: $500
- Travel. Cost $500
- Chance of Success: 50-75% average.

The Cost of Achieving 65 Percent Success For A Do-It-Yourself Hunt

Remember, our goal in this comparison is to determine the actual costs for an average hunter to achieve a 65% opportunity for success. Have a look.

- Acquisition cost of a complete elk camp including tent(s), heating stove, cooking stove, cooking equipment, water containers and water purification systems, cooking fuel, wood or gas for heat, cots, pads, tables, chairs, lanterns, and everything else under the sun that you think you have to have. Cost: $3,000 (This is conservative.)
- One first-rate mountain-ready horse. Cost: $3,000
- Annual care, feed, pasture, and maintenance for horse. Cost: $2,200+ (with no injuries)
- or one 4x4 ATV. Cost: $6,000
- Tag. Cost $500 x 5 years (to achieve 65%): $2,500
- Travel. Cost $500 x 5 years (to achieve 65%): $2,500
- Food. Cost $200 x 5 years (to achieve 65%): $1,000

As you can see, when we factor in the actual costs incurred over the time it will take the average hunter to achieve the same level of success, a fully guided-outfitted hunt is far more affordable. In addition to the actual cost savings, your learning curve as an elk hunter is much higher than starting from square one on your own.

Perhaps you are not a newbie elk hunter and already have all of your gear, a horse, ATV or method of highcountry transportation. Let's imagine for a minute that all of that was free, i.e. no cost to you (which it wasn't) but just to address that argument. You still have five years of tags, travel, and food expenses to consider. That's $6,000.... and you know that my $500 annual travel costs are extremely conservative with 2006 gas and diesel prices hovering in the $2.75 - $2.90 plus per gallon range. Also what about all that "stuff" or gear that we all buy every year. That is not included at all. In conclusion, if you want to learn a lot about elk hunting that you may not already know, and if you want to increase your chances for success by a factor of five, consider hunting with a professional outfitter at least once. If you do your homework before making the selection, you will probably have one of the best adventures of your life.

If you need help locating a reputable professional outfitter, give us a call at 719-282-4ELK (4355) or email me at elkmaster@elkcamp.com. Via our hunt consulting service, ElkCamp.com Outdoor Adventures, we have been assisting hunters just like you since 1996.

Chapter Nine

Tree Stands and Ground Blinds for Elk

A couple of years ago, a good friend and fellow elk hunter Danny Farris and I were sharing hunting stories when the subject of hunting elk from tree stands came up. I don't really remember which one of us brought the subject up first, but the ensuing discussion got me to thinking about how effective a hunting strategy it would be to use a tree stand or ground blind for elk hunting and if so, how and when would you employ it.

Because elk are such transitional animals, meaning that they typically do not always feed or bed in the same piece of real estate, and their home range, unlike whitetail deer, can cover vast tracts of land, the decision to use a fixed blind or stand is often determined as a result of thorough preseason scouting that identifies well used wallows, watering holes, or funnel-like travel routes. Funnels have long been known to Midwestern and Eastern whitetail hunters as highly productive areas that constrict the movement of game from larger tracts such like corn or soybean fields or CRP through narrow woodlots, creek beds etc., in essence funneling the game through a constricted spot enroute from one area to another. Though it flies in the face of traditional spot and stalk elk hunting methods, hanging a tree stand or setting a ground blind over or near such a point that is clearly still in use can lead to success for the hunter with the patience to wait the elk out. As any stand hunter can attest to, this type of hunting is all about patience, endurance, and one's ability to remain quiet, still, and scent free for long periods of time. By remaining in one spot, you are taking advantage of the elk's natural tendencies to move about the country.

I know… I know, Jay, you will say, you have been preaching spot and stalk, keep on the move, covering as much ground as possible for years as the most effective strategy for elk hunting. And I still do believe that, but in all fairness I figured I would be remiss if I failed to take some time to discuss other methods that can under the right circumstances produce first-rate results.

Early morning and late evening are prime times to consider hunting from a stand. As we discussed earlier, during midday, from around 10:00 am until as late as 4:00 pm elk will lay up, usually in dark timber to ruminate and rest. With large numbers of hunters moving about the woods, elk bedding areas can change from day to day, so choosing where to hang a stand in order to hunt a particular bedding area would in all likelihood be a crap shoot. However, hanging a stand or locating a ground blind near a well-used wallow or water hole can produce exceptional results for the patient hunter. Though elk do cover large distances, usually from one to four miles a day if left undisturbed, their travel patterns are fairly

ELK HUNTING 301...Making It Happen In Elk Country

predictable, and it is this predictability that might lead a stand hunter to position himself along a well used travel route as well.

Three factors that should be considered when hanging a tree stand or locating a ground blind are prevailing wind, entry and exit corridors, and clear shooting lanes. If hunting over a wallow or water source, a little investigation should reveal well traveled trails leading into and out of the area. Keep in mind that in general bull elk prefer to move towards a call that is below them; so if other factors will allow it consider placing your stand at a point lower than that from which you expect the bull to approach. Why is that? As a rule, bulls prefer to have an advantage over another bull that may be in the area and being uphill is just one such advantage. As in human warfare where armies prefer to take and hold the high ground so too do bull elk. From high ground a bull is likely to be able to see better and farther and should another bull turn up, he has the advantage of gravity on his side, i.e. charging downhill as opposed to uphill. In all my years of elk hunting, I have never been able to call a bull up a hill. Maybe your experience is different, but I for one just do not think it is going to happen. The smart hunter will not leave stand placement to chance. He understands elk behavior and uses every ounce of his skill to predict how they will enter his chosen area so that he can make it happen in elk country.

Here is a simple example. If there are well used trails coming off a higher timbered ridge to the north of the wallow and the prevailing wind is from the west, consider setting up near the bottom of the ridge near or just inside the tree line offset to the east (downwind) of the wallow.

ELK HUNTING 301...Making It Happen In Elk Country

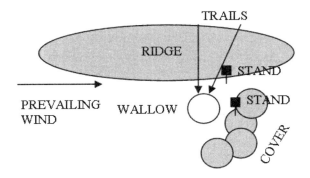

Which part of the season you hunt will determine in general where you place your stand. For Bowhunters who hunt early, consider seeking out wallows and water sources near or just below timberline near the head of a drainage. In our last book, Elk Hunting 201, my friend Roger Medley discussed hunting the backcountry carrying your bivy camp with you. Unless you have horses or mules, this may be your only option for getting into such remote country. If you elect this type of hunt, you may want to make a deal with an outfitter or local rancher with horses to help you pack out your elk. If you are hunting early in the rifle season and high enough, the elk may not have experienced the pressure that other elk farther down the mountain have experienced. In this case for the rifle hunter, a tree stand strategically placed at timberline where you can overlook a high-saddled ridge or meadows that still have some late emerging green grasses or cured grass from a previous frost may be just the ticket as elk that are less pressured may come out into the open to feed earlier in the evening while there is still good shooting light. In either case, make sure that you get a good feel for the wind and set your stand accordingly.

Tree Stands...Hangers or Climbers For Elk

For those of you unfamiliar with tree stands, there are basically two basic types: climbers or those that allow the hunter to use the stand itself to climb a tree without additional assistance using a ratcheting type motion of the upper and lower portions of the stand, and hang on or strap on stands that require the use of sticks (small lightweight portable step systems) to get up the tree and hang the stand. Each system has its advantages and limitations for elk hunting.

Over the years I have hunted out of both types of stands and found that for me climbers have a distinct advantage over hangers. They are usually far more comfortable for the hunter who plans to spend long hours up a tree as their sitting area and base platform are both typically larger than those of a hanger. I'm a pretty good-sized guy, so more room is better. Plus it's hard for me to sit anywhere for long periods of time, and if I am going to have to endure this, comfort is critical. If my backside goes numb because I have to sit on a tiny seat, or if the base is too small to allow me to stretch my legs from time to time, you can bet that I won't be in that stand for long and all that effort in stand selection will be for naught. The down side to climbers is the requirement that you must find a clean tree trunk to place them on, and when hunting elk country in most cases this means Aspen or Cottonwoods. This is not altogether a serious limitation as Aspen groves can be like elk magnets. Out west trees in the pine family such as Fir or Spruce often have thick branches that come all the way to ground level, so the idea of trying to place a climber in one of these is problematic. Actually the idea of placing any type of tree stand in a Conifer that offers little if any clear lanes for shooting is just creating work for yourself and should probably be avoided.

If the wallow or water hole that you are planning to hunt from a stand is a good ways from the truck (two miles or more), a hang on tree stand may be the better way to go as these tend to weigh considerably less, i.e. in the twelve to fourteen-pound range, than climbers which average around seventeen to twenty-pounds. There will be a tradeoff in comfort in exchange for less weight, but it may be worth it depending upon what kind of shape you are in or how far from the truck your stand is to be located.

Veteran tree stand users know this, but for those new to this type of hunting, two accessories are critical for tree stand use: a full body harness that will secure you to the tree and likely save your life in the even of a misstep, and a sturdy padlock to secure your stand to the tree when you are not around. The requirement for using a body harness is a no brainer. The padlock is to make it more of a challenge for the scoundrel that may come across your stand in the field and decide that taking your stand is a lot cheaper than buying it for himself. Unlike those misfits who stalk deer country back east looking for freebie stands, there are not too many of these walking around elk country miles from the truck with a huge set of bolt cutters. But a little forward thinking is never a bad idea.

Thinking that a great resource for information on hunting from tree stands would be from one of the most respected names in the industry, I called Paul Meeks, Founder of API Outdoors, one of the foremost manufacturers of tree stands and tree stand accessories in America about this idea of hunting elk from tree stands. Paul was very forthcoming and generous with his wisdom and insight. In the course of an informative thirty-minute conversation, Paul offered a number of nuggets of wisdom for the tree stand elk hunter, two of which really stood out in my mind as critical.

When you are considering tree stand placement try to locate the stand as centrally as possible to the water hole or travel corridor in order to minimize the possibility of elk walking into one of your shooting lanes but remaining out of effective range. For the rifle hunter this will not be as much of a limiting factor, but for the bowhunter whose maximum range may be fifty yards, a bull that comes in and remains beyond this magic shoot-no shoot boundary may as well be in another state. Paul also believes, as do I, in hunting saddles. Typically many saddles will have a meadow on one side or another. Paul suggests placing your stand on the meadow side of the saddle because experience has shown that after crossing over a saddle, elk will slow down before entering a meadow to check it out before proceeding, providing the stand hunter with the possibility of a shot at a stationary or near stationary target.

Paul suggested that I contact Jay Verzuh of Colorado Elite [Outfitters] in Grand Junction, Colorado for a second opinion on the use of tree stands for elk hunting. According to Paul, Jay has a reputation for consistently producing trophy class bulls many of which are taken from his tree stands. A quick call to Jay confirmed what Paul had said. Jay believes that tree stands are the perfect solution particularly for ambushing early season big bulls before the rut gets going. As I mentioned in Elk Hunting 201, individual bulls frequent wallows from mid-August and into early September, before they begin to form harems as they are getting worked up. Since they are not yet involved with cows, a well-placed tree stand can be the ticket to harvesting a lone big bull.

Portable Ground Blinds
Another option for stand hunting over wallows or water holes is a ground blind. In many cases, there may not be a suitable tree nearby in which to hang a tree stand or the wallow may be located in the open far from a tree line. Or you may have reached that point in life where the mere thought of climbing twenty feet up into a tree and sitting there all day is just not all that appealing. If either of these sound familiar or if you are bowhunter looking for a 50-yard or less shot, a ground blind may be a very viable option for hunting frequently used wallows or water sources in the open.

According to Brooks Johnson of Double Bull Archery, a light-weight shoot-in-any-direction ground blind like their

MatriX 360™ blind can be a very effective tool for hunting open areas that offer no concealment from the eyes of curious cows. If you are trying to put a stalk on a good herd bull, Brooks offers that the challenge is not in outsmarting the bull, it is in not getting busted by a couple of dozen sets of eyes surrounding the bull. If you can locate a water hole or wallow ahead of time, a ground blind placed within shooting range may be your ticket to success next season.

While I have hunted deer and turkey from natural ground blinds successfully for years, the concept of hunting from a portable blind like Double Bull's MatriX 360™ for elk brought a few questions to mind that I wanted to ask of one of the leaders in this industry. First and foremost I wanted to know how long it takes elk to acclimate to the presence of such a ground blind. Since elk seasons in some states can be quite limited, as short as five days in some cases, a drawn out acclimation period could be the kiss of  death for the hunter who must travel long distances to hunt and is faced with a limited season. Brooks indicated that unlike deer which do have to get used to the presence of a blind, field tests in Montana on elk demonstrate that even in open areas elk will readily walk right past a newly erected ground blind that was not there the day before with little if any regard. My second question to Brooks concerned how well the blind might help to mask a hunter's scent. Brooks responded that in cases where the wind was allowed to blow through the blind towards the elk, that whatever scent emanated from the hunter would in fact be carried on towards the elk. He quickly countered however, with the recommendation that he makes to all who ask, that Double Bull Archery recommend that no more than 180 degrees of the shooting windows of such a blind be opened at any one time, less if possible. I drew from this response that all one would need to do to prevent one's scent from being blown

ELK HUNTING 301...Making It Happen In Elk Country

down wind would be to close off the upwind windows. On the MatriX 360™, Brooks told me that all shooting ports open and close with a Silent Slide™ mechanism. If an animal circles behind the blind, and you have that side of the Surround Sight™ window system closed, you can simply open one of the four (4) silent "just-in-case" shooting ports on that half of the blind in order to get the shot without detection. A tip from the folks at Double Bull Archery for helping to manage scent is to cut some fresh sage stems or pine boughs depending up whether your blind is set up in the open flats or in the edge of timber, and lay them over the top of the blind. These freshly cut branches will emit odorous oils that will help to mask scent inside the blind.

Chapter Ten

Pass It On – The Next Generation

I once heard Dr. James Dobson once say [my paraphrase and apologies to Dr. Dobson as this is the best of my memory] that America is only one generation away from loosing its grip on our future. I took this to mean that if the current generation of Americans, parents and communities alike, does not become proactively involved in the lives of our children, our youth, if we do not exercise the leadership with which we have been charged, then the future of our country and even that of the entire planet may be in jeopardy.

Some years ago, I was talking on the phone with my dad. He was telling me how the attendance at the church that I had grown up in had dwindled over the years from what had been one of the largest churches in Memphis with thousands of

ELK HUNTING 301...Making It Happen In Elk Country

members to just a hundred or so, mostly senior citizens like himself attending on Sunday mornings. Appalled, I asked him what happened? His reply was swift and to the point, "Jay, we failed to pay attention to our youth. We were so caught up in our own generation's issues and our own lives that we failed to ensure that the generations to follow us were prepared to take over for us when we were gone." There were no future generations left to take on the roles of leadership that had sustained that great church body since the American Civil War.

I developed my love for hunting from years a field stalking Whitetail deer through hardwood lots and stands of pine in western Tennessee hunting with my dad, and he learned from those who came before him. If we want the hunting heritage that we grew up with to be available to our children and their children, then we must accept personal responsibility to ensure that heritage remains a part of our American culture. Otherwise there will be nothing for them to inherit.

The following "Tales of the Hunt" are contributed by...the next generation. As you follow along, perhaps you will see yourself or a young person you know making that journey, that right of passage from childhood to becoming a hunter. Please join with me in honoring these young men for their courage. It takes a lot of guts to write something that you know will be published for thousands to read for generations to come.

Grayson Jessen, Age 15

"I've got elk!" Ray said, as he looked through his binoculars at the enormous mountain. "How far away are they?" I asked hopefully. He replied, "Too far to shoot." The sun had already set and we had only twenty minutes of legal shooting time left on the cold 3rd day of December 2005. We began to quickly climb closer and closer. In anticipation of my first shot, sweat poured out of my body and soaked the inside layer of my camouflage which I had received for my fifteenth birthday. As I stopped to catch my breath at the top of the ridge, I saw that there were no elk. We sat on the rocks for a few anxious minutes wondering what had happened to the elk. As we headed back to camp, I felt lucky. I thought that if we saw elk the first night, I was sure to get a shot by the end of the weekend. When we returned to the camp that we had set up only a few hours before, Mrs. Money had prepared beef stroganoff for us to eat. The meal was very good, but what was better, was being with my friends and exchanging stories of the day's hunt.

"Get up!" I heard while being shaken by my best friend David. It was 4:45 a.m. time to get up eat and get ready for the adventures awaiting us. When my dad opened the tent, we saw eight inches of snow. It was very snowy and cloudy which did not make for good hunting conditions. After two cups of coffee, some biscuits and gravy, and a cinnamon roll I was ready to go.

By 6:00 a.m., we were on the go, carefully looking for any sign of elk. After a few hours of frustration at seeing nothing, Ray decided to take us to a place where we could see a lot of the thirty thousand acre ranch. "When the weather sets in, the elk go for cover, which means the dark timber. In the dark timber it is very hard to find them," Ray explained as he shifted the gears of his old Ford pickup. It was still snowing and every time it started to let up, it only got worse. We drove on and on, desperately looking for some sign of elk. Hours went by and still nothing, it just kept snowing. Then something caught my dad's eye. He said, "Look, is that a coyote?" When the large predator began to dart across the field we realized it was not a coyote. Ray said, "That ain't no coyote, that's a lion." It was. I had not ever seen a mountain lion in the wild before. Since Ray is a lion outfitter, as well as an elk guide, we sat and talked a little while about the lions around the Pikes Peak area. We then continued on the same quest as the mighty beast.

Back at camp for lunch, the menu was rattle snake and rabbit brats, which were commonly called 'fangs-n-fur." When we were done eating, us boys were assigned to split some wood. As we hacked at the dried out timber, we told each other about our day's experiences.

Josh had seen a small herd of elk only fifty yards away, but they got spooked and ran. Like me David had seen nothing since the night before. When we had finished the wood for the next night and were done with the dishes, we set out again looking for elk.

The weather didn't start to clear up until just before dark. With only thirty minutes of daylight left, we decided to head back to camp. At the last gate outside of camp I saw something on the edge of the trees. My dad said, "Oh, wait! What's that?" As Ray quietly pulled to a stop, I said, "Those are cows." I jumped out of Ray's truck and onto the snow bank. As I quickly loaded a 30-06 round into my new camo Remington 710, I loosely gripped the stock, remembering all the time I had spent in the presence of Mr. Durr learning how to be a safe, accurate hunter. I could see about eight elk through my scope as my heart pounded in my chest. Something was about to happen. So many questions raced through my mind in single moment. Should I aim high or low, to the right or the left? Which one to shoot? The one on the left is the one I had set my sights on. It was just what I had been dreaming of, a clear one hundred yard broadside shot.

As I pushed my safety off I heard Ray say, "Shoot the one on the far right." I quickly readjusted my aim. Again Ray spoke, "There are two spikes mixed in with the cows." Through my scope, I thought I saw a second elk behind the one on the far right. By the time it was confirmed, that there was not another elk, the elk were leaving and my trophy was trotting off into the timber.

In one day, I had the opportunity to see elk and a lion. It was great. We were the first hunters back at camp. I got some coffee, sat down then I told the story of my exciting day. While waiting for David and Josh I remembered the shopping day my dad and I took to get all the hunting supplies. I remembered the day the 30-06 arrived and how excited I was. Before that day I thought that hunting was only about killing an animal. But on December 4, 2005, I realized that hunting was a lot more about having fun and learning about the world that God created for us.

David returned with no elk as well, his disappointment was hard to hide. Josh was still not back, so we ate. When we had finished eating, we began to get worried. It was two hours past legal shooting time, so that meant either he was lost, stuck in a foot of snow, or he had gotten an elk. As the thermometer reached eight degrees Mr. Ray and Mr. Mathews went out to look for our unaccounted for friends. After being gone only a few minutes they returned. Mr. Mathews said, "Well, I hope they have a good fire starter." "You didn't find them!" I rudely interrupted. With a small grin Mr. Mathews replied, "We met with them on the road, they are right behind us. Josh got an elk."

A few minutes later Josh rode up in the truck. David and I ran into the cook tent to heat up the left over ribs, chicken, and fried potatoes. While they ate we listened to how Josh stalked, shot and gutted his first elk. Although David and I were a little jealous that Josh had gotten an elk and we had not yet, we were very happy for him. They finished eating and we started the dishes again, even though it was Josh's turn. "Well, we better get that skin off before it freezes," said Josh's Dad. As they were going to skin, Mr. Durr said, "You guys go help. I will finish the dishes." David and I jumped at the chance to participate and to get out of more dishes. We finished skinning and went to bed. Although I did not realize it then, that day would be one of most fun days of my fifteen years of life. I fell asleep thanking God that my hunt so far was so successful.

The next morning David again woke me up. It was the morning of the last day; I could not wait to get back out. We decided to take a short ten-minute hike down to a valley that was inaccessible in Mr. Ray's truck. When we got there, we got excited. We saw where all the elk had been. There were tracks from over one hundred elk. Tracks were going everywhere, this way and that way. We walked around in circles for 15 minutes just trying to figure out which way they had gone. It was like an elk super highway. Unfortunately, the whole day we saw nothing but that enormous assembly of elk tracks. But all was not lost, it not only was educational, it was fun just being with my Dad and Ray.

David Greenstreet, Age 15
I learned many lessons in hunting this year about how to become a better hunter. The most important thing that I learned was the Colorado rules and regulations. A second thing that I learned was the variables involved in elk hunting. I learned that the wind is a big factor while hunting. If you are not downwind from an elk they can and will most likely smell you from miles away. Scent spray and scentless detergent can help minimize a hunter's scent but not much. The elk still know you're human. I also learned to minimize the human sounds I make while walking through the woods. Things like voices, metal on metal, and clothes rubbing together are very human sounds that elk can identify from miles away.

I learned not to silhouette myself or walk straight into a clearing. Elk recognize a human silhouette really fast and they will be gone just as fast when they see a hunter. I learned that if you think you see something, don't rule it out. It might just be elk bush or it might be an elk.

The morning of December 4, 2005, our second morning in camp, the experienced hunters decided to send me to the place where my friend Josh had shot his elk the day before. We hunted all morning and were on our way back to camp when we saw elk. They were on a hillside about a mile away. We drove up around behind the hill as fast as we could and then started to stalk the elk. We were walking through the timber and I saw one through the trees, then a herd of about 30 started trotting about 20 yards in front of us. I got down on the shooting sticks that I had practiced on but the timber was so thick that I could not get a shot off. I was very disappointed but was glad to get the opportunity to get close to elk. Just before we left camp, the outfitter offered to take Grayson and I out hunting again after Christmas. We talked with Ray (Mr. Marchini) and decided to hunt the last three days of the late season, January 6, 7, and 8. I was pumped.

My dad and I woke up at 4:30 to meet Ray at 6:30 am on January 6th. We drove out to the south pasture on the ranch. As we were driving down a road I saw some elk about 800 yards away, but there were two trucks about 100 yards below them. The hunters kept on moving not even seeing the 50 elk right above them. We kept on driving since there were obviously other hunters in the area that we wanted to hunt. All we saw were deer so we went back to where we saw the elk that morning. We assumed that they were bedded down so we walked back into the timber. We were following a fresh trail when I saw something up ahead. It was brown/tan and moving fast. We kept on walking and I saw about five running to our right. We tried to sneak but the snow was so crunchy. Then another flash about 50 yards in front of us was an elk. We decided to let them calm down and come back the next day.

ELK HUNTING 301…Making It Happen In Elk Country

The next morning Mr. Matthews picked up my cousin, Kaylor and I at 5:30 am. We met Ray in Victor again and went to the south pasture. I was opening the gate when Ray spotted some elk through his binoculars. Ray and I took a radio and left one with Mr. Matthews and Kaylor back at the truck. We tried to stalk the elk but we were out in the open and they spotted us before we could get into range. We radioed Mr. Matthews back at the truck and asked him to come pick us up. We kept on the same road that we were on the day before and saw another herd on neighboring property. After that we went back to where we were the night before and glassed for more elk. We did not see anything so we went to lunch. We met my Dad, Uncle Kip, and my other cousin, Keaton, at the local deli.

After lunch Ray and I went in his truck while all of the rest piled in with Mr. Matthews. We went to two different spots in the south pasture. Mr. Matthews was looking over a big pasture, while Ray and I were watching the hill that we saw the elk on that morning. Both Ray and I did not feel good about where we were, so we decided to go to the same pasture that we saw the elk on the first day of the youth hunt.

We were driving then all of a sudden, elk. We jumped out of the truck but I could not get my sights on one. We jumped back in and drove another 50 yards and there were 30 more elk about 100 yards away. I jumped out looking for one that was not running. I missed a running elk then hundreds of them came pouring out of the trees. We ended up guessing that there were about 300 elk in that pasture. It was amazing. They all moved like one body. I was watching the elk that were not in the main herd. One stopped about 200 yards away. I drew up and shot. I thought I heard the bullet hit flesh but I was not sure. By now, there were no elk in sight. Ray had no idea I thought I hit one. He wanted to beat them to where they were going. I told him that I thought I hit one. We walked and walked all over that field but there was no blood. We decided to walk through the trees. I was about to give up when the elk jumped out of the pines and ran 10 yards. It was the one I hit. I shot it again and it dropped but it was still alive. I ended up having to shoot it two more times before it died.

I had finally killed an elk after hunting second season, the first late season, and the second late season. I was overwhelmed with joy. I was so happy. We walked back to the truck and drove off to get the other guys. By the time we got back to the elk it was dark and starting to get cold. We took pictures then gutted the elk. It was my very first elk to gut. After we were through, we put it in the back of the truck and went home to show all of my relatives and family.

The Money's, our chefs from the earlier camp, said that they had a butcher friend who wanted to come and show us how to butcher an elk. We set the time for the Wednesday after I killed the elk. We met the butcher and he showed us how to butcher the elk. We learned what different cuts of meat were and how to correctly cut them out. It was a learning and fun filled experience that I will never forget. Elk every other meal is a great thing and is pretty much how we are eating now. Even if I had not killed an elk I would still have enjoyed every minute of my experience and had a great time.

Joshua M. Steinbeiser, Age 13

My hunt of a lifetime all started on Monday, November 28, 2005 when I got home and called my Dad at work. He said, "Hey Josh, I have a surprise for you." I asked him what it was, but he wouldn't tell me. Then I got to thinking that he was going to bring pizza home. I was wrong. After he got home from work, he showed me some paper. I thought it was something related to school, but again, I was wrong. That was when he told me that I was being invited on a CDOW sponsored hunt. When he was done, he looked at me and I was sitting there with my mouth hanging wide open, thinking,

ELK HUNTING 301...Making It Happen In Elk Country

"WOW! How cool would that be?" It only took a millisecond for me to decide that I wanted to go on this hunt with my Dad. Throughout the week we packed our gear, re-packed our gear, and re-packed our gear until we had all of our stuff packed for camp. We were all ready to go, except for the most important key item. All we were missing was for me to re-qualify my rifle. Even though my rifle was completely shot in from the hundreds of rounds that went threw the barrel, we needed to make sure that it was still zeroed in. The reason for this is so that you don't go out and wound an animal. I feel that it is my responsibility and obligation to the animal that I'm shooting at, to make a good clean kill when I have the opportunity.

We arrived at base camp at 1:45 p.m. and everybody immediately started to set up camp, which took until 3:00 pm. We had some trouble putting up the tents but we got it done. As soon as we were done with the tents and the cook equipment we divided up into our hunting groups for the night hunt. As soon as everyone left, Mr. Matthews, my dad, and I went out on our hunt. We went to this valley, which had two sets of elk tracks that were fairly fresh. As we proceeded down the road we met another set of hunters that had two elk down. We talked for a little while and then followed a set of elk tracks till dark. We then were picked up by the other guide and went back to camp to eat dinner.

After dinner the other two hunters and I cleaned the dishes, there names were David and Grayson. We would joke about everything that we did. Mr. Matthews said "If you don't get the dishes done we will be eating peanut butter and jelly sandwiches three times a day." We decided that it was worth doing the dishes. That night we went to bed at 10:30 p.m.

The next morning we woke up at 4:30 in the morning, ate breakfast and then we split up into our groups again. We went to Scagway Reservoir then onto private property. We chained up on top of the ridge, and went down over the other side. We didn't see any tracks or elk so we headed back and turned up a valley called "Crazy Old Lady's Valley." Just when we weren't expecting it, my dad says "Elk!" in a louder tone then normal. We all jumped out of the truck and began a stalk. As we headed toward the hill that the elk were on, my dad and the hunt master slipped on some ice and fell. Back a little way Todd slipped on some ice too. I also slipped as we crossed a stream. Soon we were all laughing while trying to be as quiet as possible.

We started up the hill stopping to breath every few minutes. We saw the elk running in the timber on top of the hill, so we went up the valley to cut them off, but they stayed on the hilltop. We tried to approach them but as soon as we got within a 1,000 yards we saw the elk going back down the ridgeline. We decided to go back to camp for lunch.

Mrs. Melody Money was our chef who donated all the food and her time to prepare the food. Every morning she was up before all of us to make sure that we had breakfast and she was up later than all of us so she could put all of her dishes away. Lunch that day was brats that were seasoned in rattlesnake seasoning. After the delicious lunch, we all went back out for the evening hunt, but this time we had an extra person. The extra person was the hunt master's son, Henry Sorenson.

We decided to go to the spot where we had seen the herd of elk that morning. When we got there, we saw where one herd of elk had crossed over into another valley. We headed for the cross roads, when we came across a nice four point buck. We started to whistle to get it to stop. Henry pointed to the other side of the opening and said, "Elk!"

Todd turned off the truck and we all took off after the elk. We were on the opposite ridge from the elk. We stopped at a

ELK HUNTING 301...Making It Happen In Elk Country

spot that I could get a clear shot. When the elk came into view, we whistled to get them to stop, but they just wouldn't stop. We traveled through the timber and found another spot where I had a good shot, and I pulled up on the elk to take the shot, when I noticed that I couldn't see its head to determine its gender, so I didn't shoot.

We went around the basin to try sneaking up on the elk. We saw two cow elk that were just standing there. Two spikes were in front of the cows. I wanted to shoot so I waited for them to pass, and then I took the shot. My 270 went off and the boom was ringing through the air like a bomb went off. All the elk that were standing on the ridge were running like there was no tomorrow. The elk that I shot was headed down the hill. She went about half way down the hill before she stopped. I shot her eight minutes before legal shooting time was over. We got to her and she had stopped breathing. We knew that she was dead. I could feel my heart pounding in my chest from all the excitement.

We took some pictures, and headed back to the truck for our lights and knives. When we got to the basin, Todd was walking to the spot that he had heard the shot. As we were walking the path that the elk had slid down the hill, we were joking that we should charge her a slope use fee. She slid so far that it looked like a snowboard track. We got her field dressed, walked back to the truck, and we headed toward the camp. My dad had marked the point where my elk was on his GPS. After we field dressed my elk and got to the truck, the day had worn away, we couldn't see the stars because of the dark and dreary clouds. That night, the night air was so cold that we thought that the elk would freeze solid. My dad said, "We should just drag her down the hill now instead of in the morning." They dragged her down the hill, but they missed the spot where the truck was by half of a mile. While Mr. Sorenson and I waited in the truck for Mr. Weeda, Henry, and my Dad dragged the elk to the truck, Mr. Sorenson taught me how to fill out my hunting license correctly. We moved the truck down the road that extra half-mile.

Once we had her in the back of the truck we headed to camp. When we got back to camp everyone was congratulating me. After we ate dinner, we talked about how to skin an elk. All the hunters washed the dishes and headed outside to skin my elk but it was so cold that my dad and Mr. Weeda skinned her. After that we all went into our sleeping tents and went to bed. That night was the coldest night that I had ever spent out in the wilderness.

The next morning when all the hunters were out, whoever was left at camp helped take down camp. After camp was all packed away, we waited for the others to come back. As soon as Mr. Marchini got back to camp with Grayson, they told everyone that they had seen a mountain lion a couple hundred yards away. I thought that was probably the coolest experience that anyone could have. I know people that have spent years in the woods and have never seen a mountain lion. Once everyone was back at camp, we all took pictures of the camp crew. After we took the pictures and got everyone out of the camping area, my dad, Mr. Marchini, Mr. Weeda and I went to a restaurant called "Zeks Place" that serves some of the biggest burgers in town. We all said our farewells, and my Dad and I drove home. This hunt was such a wonderful experience that I would do it again, no matter the time, no matter the conditions. I appreciate the efforts that everybody put forth for this hunt. It truly was a hunt of a lifetime.

Chapter Eleven

Thoughts From A Woman Hunter

Vickie Gardner

I am a woman who hunts...I love how that sounds. I love what it means. In 2005 I was blessed with the opportunity to go on my first hunt, not as a spectator along for the ride, but as a participant in an adventure that has been a part of mankind since before time was recorded. I was...a hunter. What a remarkable opportunity, a former tree-hugging granny hunting? Yes for many reasons. It provides me with a chance to share with

my grandchildren, my Godchildren, girlfriends, husband and family the joy and thrill of hunting. To share what I've learned is the "circle of life."

I was born into a loving but non-hunting California tree-hugging family. Growing up I never knew a hunter or anyone who participated in the shooting sports. In my world, television cowboys fought off the bad guys with guns, or in war movies, soldiers were depicted surrounded by bomb blasts or the enemy swooning from a wound from a machine gun; more often it was cops and robbers shooting each other. Sometimes our family watched movies portraying the life of early American pioneers who had to hunt in order to survive. These films rarely showed any of the real-life aspect of the hunt beyond the shot and the smoke from the hunter's flintlock rifle. We never saw the backbreaking work required of the hunter as he field dressed his deer, or how he actually got the game back to his family. Well, there was this one scene where the successful hunter dressed in fringed buckskin strolled up to the homestead without a lick of sweat or dirt on his duds, a dead doe draped across his shoulders. Yeah, I bet he walked a few miles like that. I don't think so! The word around our home as I was growing up was "Guns are frightening, and if we even got near a gun we might likely get killed or at the least badly hurt." That's how my siblings and I and everyone I knew were raised. I accepted that commonly held doctrine without question, for I had other pressing factors to deal with.

I was born to be a mother, a teaching, nurturing, outdoorsy mama. In accordance with my own upbringing, I passed my ignorance of guns on to my three daughters. When I shot my first gun at a writer's conference, I was already a grandma and to be honest I was not too excited to be holding such a powerful and dangerous weapon.

ELK HUNTING 301...Making It Happen In Elk Country

Eventually I decided to enroll in a shooting class. I followed the instructor's rules to the letter. Imagine my surprise when I actually hit those little flying orange things? I actually thought that someone else was shooting them for me! That day something happened to me, something changed within me, and I kept on shooting and shooting. I loved it!

I won a gun that day and placed a call to our daughters. The conversation went something like this: "Hi, this is Mom...I won a GUN!" One of my girls exclaimed "Mom...what on earth are you gonna do with it?" I said, "Shoot it." My daughter explained, "But Mom that goes against everything you've ever taught us." I humbly replied, "I was wrong and I'm sorry, but I'm going be making my grandkids elk tacos in a few years!"

Today I am a woman who now owns guns and I hunt whenever I get the chance. I'm so very grateful to be able to share that fact, knowing that I now have the chance to start my own family traditions in the shooting sports. This need for establishing these new hunting traditions came to light recently when my 17-year-old Godson asked me if I ever went hunting and if so, would I take him? My husband Tim and I own Alpen Optics, so hunting is a rather significant part of our business. My Godson Ryan must have just assumed I liked the idea of hunting. Over the past year I have met some delightful hunting families with rich hunting traditions. I'd even watched a movie called "The Sacred Hunt" that actually made sense to me. Earlier in my life as a teacher I had a heartfelt curiosity about hunting and would discuss these issues with my class. In recent years through our business I have been blessed to meet sweet intelligent women who are hunters. Though I was in such awe of them, I never really saw myself as a hunter.

When our 13-year-old Goddaughter Jenny was released from the City of Hope Hospital having survived a year of cancer treatment, her brother Ryan asked me out of the blue to take him hunting. I remember smiling and telling him "no problem," but my brain yelled.... "What are you saying?" "You barely have time to breathe"... "How and where will you learn to hunt?".... "You big fibber!" That was Christmas Eve, 2004. In January, 2005 at the Shot Show (after spending sleepless nights pondering and praying about that fib) I had no other choice but to learn to hunt. Maybe it's because I am a woman, but my nurturing spirit kicked in hard and I realized that if I didn't take Ryan hunting, who would? I had the connections and maybe I wasn't too old to learn to hunt. By Shot Show 2005 my husband knew that I was on the brink of stepping into an adventure I wasn't sure of, and didn't know if I could pull off. His response to my concerns was confident and sweet. He hugged me and told me get out there and bring home the bacon cus' he was a great cook.

Sharing my desire to learn to hunt with a few people at that show I was literally overwhelmed with the response. A bunny-loving, granola-crunching, spider-saving, granny willing to go over to the dark side...to the world of guns, blood, death and camo. The folks at the show couldn't wait to get me in the woods and show me how it's done. "Now hold on fluffy!" I think that's what I said. I'm only shooting what we can eat and I want to learn from the most ethical people who love the animal as much as the hunt.

Is this the voice of a woman or it this the voice of the new hunter? How does that make me different than a man? To be honest a few of my closest men friends told me I could never kill an animal. I told them I wouldn't know until the time comes. Some men told me stories of wounded animals and I vowed that I would not injure an animal. I would not shoot until I knew in my heart of hearts that it was a good shot, a safe shot, and an ethical shot. Does that make me any different then a guy hunter? No...I think most male hunters feel the same as I do.

ELK HUNTING 301...Making It Happen In Elk Country

I arranged to take my Godson, Ryan Huffman on a Kansas turkey hunt with an outfitter friend, Gene Pearcy of Kansas Whitetail Adventures TV. To prepare myself for the upcoming hunt I found a wonderful shooting teacher, Sheila Link who in a very short time taught me to shoot. Thank God Sheila agreed to go with Ryan and I on the hunt sharing her advice and turkey hunting wisdom with us both.

The first three days of my first ever hunt began early each morning in the pre-dawn hours with Ryan and I and the other hunters joining in the "hunting ritual." Up early in the cold and dark whispering and laughing at bad jokes, drinking lots of steaming coffee trying to stay alert while settling the adrenaline butterflies in our bellies. Trying to remain quiet we sneaked over the dark morning ground bundled from head to toe in camo with tiny flashlights lighting the way and big guns hoisted upon our shoulders. As we waited patiently sitting in the blind or lying against an old log, it seemed as if we hardly breathed trying as hard as we could to be quiet and not give ourselves away to the turkeys roosting nearby. Hearing the turkeys fly down from their roosts directly over our heads was electrifying and spiritual at the same time. The most wonderful words I heard that entire week were from Ryan after we had been out in the field in 32-degree weather since 5:00 am. He turned and looked at me through his camo facemask and whispered, "Vickie, if we flew out here all the way from CA and all we got to do is this...it's GREAT! As fate would have it, Ryan is the only one who bagged a turkey that week and he nailed it just four hours before our plane was to leave. When our guide prayed "Thank you God for this beautiful bird," I knew Ryan had been blessed with a true hunting experience and a life long memory.

Since that first hunt I've traveled to South Dakota to shoot prairie rats (ground hogs), south to Texas for Axis Deer (and a TV show), around the globe to Africa for Wildebeest, to Maui for another Axis Deer hunt, and finally to Alabama for

Whitetail. To top it off as I write this I am getting ready for a spring turkey hunt in Texas. What have I learned? Respect for wildlife. Respect for good hunters and ethical sportsmen. I am dedicated to becoming a good hunter – a true sportswoman. Taking an animal's life humbles me and at the same time fills my heart with appreciation for that animal.

My hope is that watching me learn to hunt will intrigue and maybe even inspire my family and friends to think about hunting, to have a curiosity about hunting, to get educated about firearms and possibly even realize the fun of shooting sports for themselves. I want to take my grandkids hunting and even if it doesn't evolve to become the family tradition I dream of, I hope that at the least they will learn from me to respect the world of hunting. Does this thinking make me any different then a man who hunts? I don't think so.

If you want to start a family tradition like hunting, you'd be better off starting sooner than later! My female hunting mentor Sheila, has been happily married for fifty years to a non-hunter who though he has questioned her love of guns and shooting sports, he still supports and cheers her on. I just started hunting nine months ago and I only have 42 more years until I'm 100, so I have a lot to do!

Chapter Twelve

A Country Elk Hunter Speaks

Phil Weaver

Phil Weaver is a long time die-hard elk hunter and a great personal huntin' buddy of mine. I have had the privilege of sitting around more than one campfire in elk country listening to Phil's years of wisdom spun in his native Arkansas color and drawl. Phil writes like he talks and I have tried my best to maintain as much of Phil's essence as possible. If you're not from down Phil's way you may have to pay close attention to catch the nugget that Phil is tossing out. Let's hear from Ol'Arky. (He doesn't really talk like this. He just likes folks to think he does.)

If I Was A Elk Where Would I Be?

If I was a elk where would I be and what would I be doin' right now? This is a question most ever' elk hunter ought to ask himself when they arrive in elk country. Not a week before… not a day or so after, but as soon as ya arrive and see for yaself the conditions ya have to contend with. If I was a elk is the start of every scoutin' trip and elk hunt I've ever had the privilege of goin' on. Ya gotta find 'um before ya kill 'um.

Elk on Colorado public land are a bit different than elk in Rocky Mountain National Park or Yellowstone Park. The elk in those two areas are more than likely the most photographed elk in the USA. They even pose for ya or so I'm told. So let's don't even consider them.

Elk in the wilds are a bit different and have to do a few things different. If they pose for ya very long they likely won't live to see the next sunrise durin' huntin' season. Let me say this first and foremost, just because this is what I would do and where I would look doesn't mean it's the only way to do it or the only place to look for elk. There's more than one way to skin a cat.

With that said, I look for elk from high to low. I get as high as I can (that's speaking of elevation folks, not drugs) and look for 'um below me. There ain't no reason for me to look higher 'cause I'm as high as I can get. The reason I like to go high and look low is you can see better lookin' down into an area than tryin' to look up from down low. Ya can see into the dark timber and aspen groves. Ya can see where these two meet and that is important to ya and the elk. Elk love to be in some sorta cover durin' the hours ya can legally hunt 'um. Dark timber for when it's hot or they are getting' a lota pressure and cool aspen when they are hungry or thirsty.

In most aspen areas you are gonna find some sorta water if ya look hard enough for it. The elk already know where it is. So I just try to follow elk sign to find it. I always used to make mental notes of where those areas where, but now I gotta make written notes 'cause I can't remember as well anymore, and I think that's a better way to do it anyway. The areas I look for are areas that have what elk need on a day-to-day basis. I look for aspen borderin' dark timber, benches, drainage heads, saddles that the elk use for escape routes, most anything that has some type of cover. All these areas can be located BEFORE ya put ya boots on the ground by lookin' over aerial photos, which are available to any a ya on the Internet.

Maps and MapCard

If ya don't have a computer then it's a bit harder but they are a valuable resource to anyone that hunts anythin'. I use MapCard, a service available at www.mapcard.com which cost less than twenty bucks a year, and it gives me access to topo maps and aerial photos of most anywhere I'll ever hunt. Paper maps whether they are the ones ya print or ones ya buy are somethin' ya need to have with ya while scoutin' or huntin'. Everthin' I see that I wanta remember I mark on my map. I use a GPS and it has plenty a stored waypoints. The reason I use MapCard is it will put me within a very short distance of any spot I'm interested in lookin' at. It has a function where ya mouse over the map and it shows the GPS coordinates for the location ya mouse is pointed at. It has a zoom feature and by usin' that zoom and the mouse I can find the exact location after manually puttin' it into my GPS. But any good map software will do the same thing. I also use DeLorme TOPO USA. Like I said, I like to know what I'm getting' into before I get there. I only have a short period of time to find elk once we arrive. If I lived in elk country, I'd spend more time in and amongst 'um.

Aspen bordered by dark timber: These are areas used by elk all day long if it ain't too hot and the predator pressure is not too heavy. The Aspen on the aerial photos show up a bit lighter in color than the dark timber Spruce and Pine. If they are where a bench starts or ends so much the better. For those that don't know a bench ain't somethin' ya set on in the park, it's an area on the side of a ridge that is flatter than the rest a the slope. I guess that's why we call 'um benches. They are a good place to rest when goin' up or down the side a that ridge and a good place to find elk also. Elk ain't dumb. They like to use the course of least resistance durin' normal day-to-day travel from point A to point B. But they will go up the side of a mountain in a heartbeat if ya put too much pressure on 'um. These benches can be found on a topo map by lookin' for where the contour lines get wider apart on the side of the ridge or mountain. Here's a little secret about topo maps for the high country. The contour lines are at larger intervals than topo maps for flatter country. Another secret, in most any area that appears pretty flat, there are places a mature bull elk can use that will hide 'um from ya even though ya think ya oughta be able to see 'um. Little ridges or depressions that are eight to ten feet high or deep DO NOT show up on topo maps. That's the reason for boots on the ground and eyes in the timber scoutin'. Ya gotta find those places. Elk know where they are. You should too. They will do one of two things. They will protect the elk OR give ya the advantage a seein' 'um. An ADVANTAGE is a word a lota folks don't use, 'cept those that kill elk on a regular basis. Any advantage ya can get on 'um is a lot better than any advantage ya give to 'um. They got plenty anyway. Why give more. Saddles are just a pretty good size depression on a ridge top that if viewed from the side looks like the seat area of a saddle. Elk use saddles. They love 'um. In good elk country ya will find elk trails in saddles goin' from one side of the mountain to the other. Never overlook a saddle. I look at ever' one I can find. Drainages can be anythin' from just a slight depression goin' downhill to a full blown river and anythin' in between. I like the anythin' in between. There's a lot more of 'um and elk love to follow those littl' gems. A drainage within a saddle is "THE SPOT." If I ever find one I'll live there for the season if there are elk in the area. There will be elk using that saddle sometime durin' the season if they are there and movin' from one side a that mountain to the other side a it. The amount of fresh sign will tell ya if ya need to be there or not.

Summer Scoutin'
I'm gonna switch gears here for a minute and talk 'bout summer boots on the ground and eyes in the timber scoutin. Durin' summer scoutin' trips I always use my handy dandy spottin' scope and look way up high for big bull elk since they spend mosta their time there tryin' ta stay cool. Herds a elk in the summer mainly consist of a cow, calves and young bulls. They can be found most anywhere BUT the big guys are normally up high where it is cooler and more comfortable for 'um. Coolness and comfort is all important to 'um while grownin' those big antlers we all have dreams of. This is about the only time I want to get as high as I can get and look down. But even durin' the summer I'll get high and look down when lookin' for elk herds and smaller bulls. I like to see elk when scoutin' durin' the summer and the higher you look the more ya see 'cause it's more open above timberline and the elk are up there 'cause the groceries are up there.

I used to walk a lot of closed roads durin' my summer scoutin' trips but with age and my medical condition slowin' me a bit I just stumble 'um a bit. Any place I can see for a long way I'll stop and look. I use to really like closed and/or gated roads but now days folks can't seem to read as good as they used too so the closed roads are not as effective as they used to be but I still use 'um.

What causes a elk to do what they do? SURVIVAL! Elk live day to day to survive to the next day. They don't have anythin' that they gotta do except eat, drink, sleep and survive. They ain't gotta be here today and there tomorrow. No appointments to keep. All they gotta do is survive.

Here's another opinion. The only reason elk migrate outa the high country or the area they call home is the lack of groceries or predator pressure. The lack of groceries may be caused by drought, overgrazin', deep snow cover, etc. If ya only get one thing from this chapter this needs to be it. Larger bull elk will be the last to leave their home area. Snow alone will not force elk outa the high country. The lack of groceries is what moves elk outa the high country. Heavy predator pressure can also cause elk to migrate. Predator pressure can come in many forms; a large amount a predators in an area; intrusion of humans to name a few. The more predators (human or natural) in a given area the less elk will be in or around that given area. Now ya see why I said ya gotta forget the elk in Rocky Mountain National Park and Yellowstone Park. These elk are not hunted by humans, only by natural predators. And the natural predators are not as common in those areas. In those areas elk have no fear of humans. Humans help 'um more than they hurt 'um. But wild elk that are hunted by humans have that fear. The elk that don't have the fear of man don't live very long lives. We humans cause elk to relocate more than natural predators. Humans and natural predators are both "selective" hunters. The difference here is that humans pray on the strong and most vigorous while natural predators prey on the young and weak. Mature elk can protect 'umself from natural predators but not from humans other than to get the heck outa Dodge. Thus when the human predator arrives on the scene elk get ants in their pants. They just gotta find someplace else, someplace without all 'um pesky humans and the sharp sticks and thunderbolts. I would too if almost every time I came in contact with a human one a my buddies came up MIA.

So if I was a elk, where would I be durin' huntin' season? Where human predators ain't. That's kinda simple but it's the truth. Elk that ain't are normally in those same human predator's freezers cut up nicely into steaks and ground in to sausage and elk burger.

Elk Comfort Zones
So let's look at the areas elk prefer that are not where humans prefer. The nastiest, darkest, hardest to get to hellhole ya can find. A place where when ya kill an elk (and ya will kill one if ya go there) it will take ya the better part a ya hunt to get him out of. But not all elk do that. Remember this… a lota elk only go as far as they have to, to get away from those pesky humans. Might be a half-mile. Might be five miles. But when elk get in that comfort zone they will stay until 1) they run outa groceries or 2) predators invade that comfort zone. Elk comfort zones can be just over that ridge that has a rock face or rockslide and is hard for humans to get to. That ridge might only be half-mile from the nearest road but elk feel secure because no humans have ever invaded that area. Another place is small stands of timber (cover) in open areas or a small stand a dark timber in open aspen areas. If elk think ya can't see 'um YA CAN'T SEE 'UM. I've seen hunters walk past elk that are in open aspen areas and never know an elk was there. Durin' my summer scoutin' trips it never fails that I'm on a well-used road watchin' elk, and up pulls some nice folks. I'm standin' outside my ol' Dodge truck with only my binoculars hangin' on my neck. We exchange "Hi… How are ya's." and then without fail these words come outa their mouth. "Seen anythin' today?" It happens ever year and sometimes more than once. I'm nice and don't fib very much and just say "A few here and there." Ya see I didn't fib very much 'cause I told 'um here. Folks

sometimes can't see the forest for the trees or vise versa but they need to be able to "see the trees in the forest." That's how I see elk. I LOOK FOR 'UM. I don't look for a big ol' fat 6x6 trophy bull elk standin' in the broad open. I look for somethin' that ain't supposed to be there. In a forest ya got trees, scrubs, logs and a few other things that are there all the time. Then ya got elk or deer or whatever that is there part a the time. They don't look like trees or scrubs or logs. They look DIFFERENT. A patch a tan, a flash, a movement, Radar ears or eyes. They got 'um and ya need to have 'um too. Lookin' for somethin' that ain't supposed to be there has found me a lota critters that I wouldn't have found if I was lookin' at the forest or the trees. Same holds true durin' huntin' season. If ya train your eyes not to look at somethin' but to look for somethin' ya will see more critters.

I'm gonna make some a ya mad but think on this a bit. Durin' a scoutin' trip or huntin' trip more elk will see you then you see them.

WAO………. Too many folks go WAO when scoutin' or huntin'. What is WAO? Wide A (the cousin of a donkey) Open. Slow down and you'll see more critters. Be like 'um. They ain't got no place they gota be. Neither should ya. Just go with what got ya there. Slow and easy, always lookin'. And in the case a elk smellin'. Don't listen to that commercial "forget the wind just hunt". If ya hunt with the wind in ya face ya will smell more elk before ya see 'um. If ya forget the wind and just hunt, well remember what I said about more elk seein' ya than ya seein' them? Same holds true here only difference is they will smell ya. An elk will stand and stare at somethin' they ain't sure of, but if they smell a human on it, ADIOS AMIGO. After my heart attack and quitin' smokin', I found out my sense of smell is a lot better than my sense a hearin'. Elk have a unique odor. Once ya smell 'um ya won't forget it. I wish I could describe it for ya but I can't. But ya'll know when ya are smellin' elk. Again here it is a musty odor in the air that just ain't supposed to be there. Elk can hear ya near 'bout as good as they can smell ya. Fool 'um, make 'um think ya are another elk or critter. This goes along with not goin' WAO through elk country The only time when elk go WOA is when they know that ya know they are there. Elk are masters of the art of hidin' in plain sight. They just have the knack of knowin' when they've been discovered. So use all ya senses. Elk do. It's all about advantage. If ya don't use ya senses when huntin' elk, it's like showin' up with a knife at a gunfight. Just ain't that smart a thing to do. Hunt smart.

I hope this will help a few a ya in ya pursuit of the great wapiti. These critters we chase are majestic critters and fun to be in and amongst. Getting' in and amongst 'um is what it's all about. After the shot, the fun ends and the work begins. But it is a labor of love. At least it is in my case.

See ya out there,
Phil "Ol' Arky" Weaver

Chapter Thirteen

Quartering Your Elk Without Field Dressing

In Elk Hunting 201 we walked you through the conventional method of field dressing your elk. Now we want to show you another method that many experienced elk hunters have switched to. Not only will this method save you time, and effort, but also it is far less messy and you will not have to worry about dealing with the gut.

Tools & Stuff
Start with a quality sharp hunting knife (two is better) with strong blades and no-slip handles. This is another one of those times you really don't want to go cheap as many inexpensive imported knives are made of low-grade steel that

doesn't want to hold an edge and can break with only a minor amount of lateral pressure to the blade. Benchmade, Buck, Gerber, Kershaw, SOG, and Spyderco make excellent hunting knives. You will also need a sharpening stone. I carry a folding diamond dust sharpener and a small ceramic V-shaped sharpener for quick jobs. If you need to do some serious knife sharpening, you can't beat a Lansky sharpening system. Mine has three separate hones. They take up a little more room, but when it comes to getting the job done on almost any knife, they are tough to beat. You will want to have a lightweight saw for removing the skullcap if you decide to take the antlers home without the entire head. To round out your gear you will need four or five heavy-duty cotton game bags, and about 50 feet of nylon cord. If you can afford to spend a few extra bucks, you can get ultra-low stretch cord at many backpacker shops like REI or EMS. This really comes in handy back at camp when it's time to hang your game up to cool and keep away from critters. I've had some of the less expensive cord stretch out during the night due to the weight and find the game bag hanging substantially lower than where I left it the night before. It's your call.

Kevin Fair easily packs out a quarter on his Wolf Pack Systems pack.

Let's Get 'Er Done

1. Roll the elk onto its side and position its feet heading downhill. If the animal is on a slope and you need to stabilize it, use the 50-feet of cord to tie it off to a nearby tree or a good-sized rock.
2. Using your knife make a cut through the hide from just behind the elk's skull down the spine all the way to the tail.
3. Make another cut through the hide just behind the scapula (shoulder blade) around to the brisket.
4. Skin the shoulder. Some prefer to leave the hide on to keep out the dirt until putting the shoulder into a meat bag. I prefer to remove the hide as soon as possible to begin cooling the meat down and preventing bacteria growth from kicking into high gear. Either way works, it's your call.

5. Lift the leg and remove the shoulder and place in a game bag.
6. Remove as much rib and neck meat as you desire. This is where a fifth game bag comes in handy.
7. Skin the hindquarter on this side and remove by cutting against the pelvic bone until you reach the joint. Cut remaining tendons and ligaments and place in a game bag.
8. Remove the back straps by cutting down the spine from head to tail and peeling this piece away from the spine and upper ribs. Place in game bag.
9. Remove the tenderloins - located inside the carcass on either side of the spine - by either cutting through the tops of the ribs or by pulling them free by reaching under the spine between the ribs. Place in game bag.
10. Flip the animal over and repeat the process.
11. If you have a long way to pack out your animal, you may want to bone out the quarters right on the spot and remove the lower legs at the joint with your saw to save having to haul the extra weight back to camp.

There you have it, one elk in bags without most of the mess, stink and fuss of having to field dress it.

Chapter Fourteen

Hot New Gear For Elk Hunters

In each volume of our Elk Hunting series we feature a brief look at gear that we believe can make a measurable difference in your elk hunting adventure. While there are many excellent products on the market, we believe that these are the "best of the best."

Alpen Optics "Ranier™" Binoculars

If you are looking for the best affordable binocular for elk hunters on the market, take a look at the new Alpen Rainier™ binocular series available in both 8x42 and 10x42. I have been using Alpen binos for years. These binoculars provide the best optical and mechanical craftsmanship available today. From the rugged magnesium body to the ultra precision ground and polished optical elements, Rainier™ delivers the best premium-performance. All optical components receive Alpen's exclusive UBX™ multi-layer coating for maximum light transmission. The extra large BaK-4 prisms are coated with Alpen's SHR™ metallic  and PXA™ phase coatings to deliver the best in brightness, clarity and color fidelity. Large diameter lens elements throughout the optical system provide enhanced field of view and eye relief for easy viewing.

Rainier binoculars are extremely rugged yet precise optical instruments to provide years of reliable performance. The textured rubber covering design is durable yet comfortable. The tightly o-ring sealed nitrogen filled body ensures complete water proof and fog proof protection against anything mother nature can throw at it. I have hauled my Alpen's all over Colorado, Idaho, and Montana in every conceivable type of weather from blowing rain and snow to extreme summer temps and not once have they ever failed to perform as expected. Before you buy your next set of binoculars or a spotting scope give Alpen Optics a try.

Contact:
Alpen Optics
10329 Dorset Street
Rancho Cucamonga, CA 91730
(909) 987-8370
www.alpenoutdoor.com

MapCard™

Building on the success of its custom map products, MyTopo has introduced a new do-it-yourself mapping service available via annual subscription for $19.95, or $29.95 for the pro level. Simple Internet-based mapping tools allow access to MyTopo's entire database of over 300,000 maps and aerial photos, with roads and highways and a public land survey system overlay options. Subscribers can quickly and easily design and print unlimited mini navigation-ready maps on 8.5" x 11" and 11" x 17" paper. They can also download maps for use in other programs, or save maps on the system, making their own library of maps available to them from any computer with Internet access. The service has an easy to use set of drawing and measuring tools for marking up maps. Users can draw trails, precisely outline areas, add symbols, and even measure distances and acreage. GPS users can upload and download waypoints and tracks onto their maps.

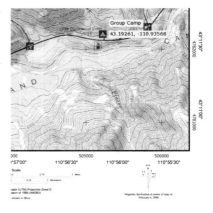

MyTopo's subscription service is a great investment for people who use maps for their outdoor activities and for desktop scouting. It's also an important safety precaution for people who regularly visit the backcountry. Subscribers can make a map of the area they plan to hunt, using the tools to denote where they will park and camp, and leave copies with local law enforcement and loved ones so they always know where you are.

You can access this great new mapping service via our website at www.ElkCamp.com. click on **Hunting Maps**. If you have questions give the folks at MyTopo a call.

Contact:
Paige Darden, Marketing & Public Relations
(866) 587-9015
Web: www.mytopo.com
Email: paige@mytopo.com

Sitka Mountain Gear™

For years I have been waiting for someone to develop high-performance or what I like to call smart gear; or hunting clothing that incorporates leading edge technology in the areas of layering, insulation, water resistance, sound reduction, and camouflage. An architect or engineer will confirm that a basic rule of

thumb in design is that form should follow function. In recent years however, the hunting apparel industry seems to have focused much of its effort on form, i.e. what the product looks like and less effort on how the garment actually performs...or function. Even though a majority of industry professionals, and writers like myself continue to hammer layering as a preferred strategy for hunting clothing, the manufacturers, for the most part, have continued to produce heavy and bulky hunting clothing products. Until now...enter two youthful yet really smart outdoorsmen, Jason Hairston and Jonathan Hart, co-owners of Sitka Mountain Gear™.

Jason and Jonathan had a simple goal: to introduce to the hunting industry a system of clothing that incorporates the latest high-performance fabrics with a mountaineering design philosophy. Sitka has created a line of clothing that is designed to perform under the various circumstances that hunters find in the mountains, while hiding them with an extremely effective, multi-season pattern called Mountain Mimicry. Sitka Mountain Gear™ is based on the tried-and-true system of layering, which gives the hunter the flexibility needed for hunting in the mountains. Sitka offers a moisture-wicking base layer, warm thermal layer and quiet and tough DWR-finished outer layer that is based on Soft Shell Technology. This allows you to climb light when you are heating up and to control your temperature when you are slowing down or when the weather changes.

The true strength of a layering system is in the individual pieces. Collectively, the combination of every layer gives you a system that performs better than anything possible. Each individual layer, whether it's your base layer, vest, or outer layer, all play very specialized roles. Each excels in different climates, designed for different needs. By using the most advanced weaves, fabrics, and designs, each layer packs easily and is very lightweight, allowing you to travel light, without compromising protection from the elements. This is the foundation for the Sitka System. If you think that performance should be the measure of quality gear, consider Sitka Mountain Gear™ next time you are in the market for hunting apparel. I have. Look for Sitka Mountain Gear™ in our upcoming **THE ELK HUNTER SERIES** DVD, available October 2006.

Contact:
Jason Hairston, VP
240 South First Street
Dixon, CA 94941
(916) 804-5726
Web: www.sitkagear.com
Email: jhairston@sitkagear.com

Double Bull Archery Matrix 360°™

In chapter nine I talked about how Double Bull Archery's Matrix 360°™ ground blind may be the solution to ambushing that bull that you have patterned to be using a waterhole regularly. Here is the real skinny on this awesome blind. The Matrix 360°™ features patented Surround Sight™ Technology — the first and only blind that erases forever the "limited visibility" disadvantage. Offering unsurpassed viewing adjustability — up to 5,520 square inches of window area — and all of the time tested features that have made Double Bull Archery's premium blinds famous. The Matrix 360°™ redefines the ground blind.

You must be able to see, but not be seen; and until now, the problem with ground blinds has been the window. A ground blind conceals the hunter by limiting the amount of light entering the blind. However, the problem was that opening and closing small, individual windows used to severely restrict visibility. Now, with Matrix's patented continuous Surround Sight™ window system around the full circumference of the blind, you can achieve maximum visibility with minimum light entering the blind. The result? You see the game; the game doesn't see you. You get the game!

Now you can open one, two, three or all four sides of the blind depending on conditions. You can open a side from as little as 1 inch across to as much as 23 inches. No more dead space. You can slide the window opening up or down thanks to the Silent Slide™ system and set it to the exact location for your own height, the height of your chair, and the lay of the land. And, you can use the integrated shoot-through, drop-down netting, or easily secure it out of the way.

ELK HUNTING 301...Making It Happen In Elk Country

If an animal circles behind the blind, and you have that side of the Surround Sight™ window system closed, you can simply open one of the four (4) silent "just-in-case" shooting ports on that half of the blind in order to get the shot without detection.

Add in their exclusive patented adjustable framework, generous 6-foot plus shooting diameter, exclusive Predator Deception ground blind-specific camo, and custom cotton/poly black-backed weatherproof fabric, and it all adds up to the ultimate ground blind from the ultimate ground blind manufacturer. Step inside a Matrix 360™, pull up a chair, adjust the Surround Sight™ continuous window to your liking, and you'll gain an instant appreciation for our "Big Picture" approach to manufacturing premium hunting blinds.

Double Bull Archery's reputation for producing first-class ground blinds is undisputed in the industry. Next time you are in the market for the ultimate in ground blinds check out Double Bull Archery.

Contact:
Double Bull Archery
P.O. Box 923
Monticello, MN 55362
(888) 464-0409
Web: www.doublebullarchery.com
Email: muskiebrx@aol.com

References

Elk of North America; Ecology and Management, Thomas & Toweill, Stackpole Books, Harrisburg, PA, 1982

Elk Country, Valerius Geist, Northword Press, Minocqua, MN, 1993

Elk, Behavior, Ecology, and Conservation, Edwin and Peggy Bauer, Voyageur Press, Stillwater, MN, 1995

Elk Hunt, A Complete Guide by one of America's Foremost Hunting Writers, Jim Zumbo, Winchester Press, Clinton, NJ, 1985

Elk and Elk Hunting, Hart Wixon, Stackpole Books, Harrisburg, PA, 1986

The Complete Book of Elk Hunting, Sam Curtis, The Lyons Press, Guilford, CT, 2005

Elk Essentials, Bob Robb, The North American Hunting Club, 1999

The Elk Hunter, Don Laubach and Mark Henckel, Falcon Publishing, Inc, Helena, MT, 1989

Boone & Crockett Club website, http://www.boone-crockett.org

Pope and Young Club website, http://www.pope-young.org

Safari Club International website, http://www.safariclub.org

About the Author

Elk Hunting 301, Making It Happen In Elk Country is Jay Houston's third and final book in his series on the diverse and challenging aspects of elk hunting. His first book on this subject, *Elk Hunting 101, A Pocketbook Guide to Elk Hunting* released by Jackson Creek Publishers in the Spring of 2004 quickly became the fastest selling new book on elk hunting in America. His second highly successful book *Elk Hunting 201, Big Bulls...Essentials for a Successful Hunt* was released in August 2005 and like Elk Hunting 101 is now available across America via major booksellers and better sporting goods retailers. Jay's books have received wide acclaim from professionals throughout the elk and big game hunting industries. Jay works closely with the Rocky Mountain Elk Foundation as a speaker at its Annual Elk Camp. He travels and speaks extensively about elk hunting and elk country. He is frequently asked to attend RMEF chapter banquets where he visits with fellow elk hunters and sales of his books are used as fundraisers for the RMEF chapter. Jay's Elk Hunting series has helped thousands of elk hunters and would-be elk hunters become more knowledgeable about this great adventure we call elk hunting.

A life-long big game hunter, national conference speaker on elk and elk hunting, hunting agent, editor and writer Jay has taken his passion for hunting and the outdoors and combined these with his fervent desire to pass on the knowledge and skill that he and others have acquired to those who will follow.

Email: elkmaster@elkcamp.com

About the Cover Photographer
Jerry Gowins Jr.

Jerry Gowins Jr. is an award-winning photographer from Eugene, Oregon. An avid bowhunter, his passion for the hunt and all things wild has led him to hunting as much with his camera as his bows. In 1989, Jerry sold his first magazine cover to Traditional Bowhunter Magazine. In 2004, Jerry became a acknowledged Regular Contributor to the magazine. To date Jerry has sold more than twenty-five cover photos and he has penned a basic photography column for Traditional Bowhunter Magazine, as well as several serious and humor articles. Rumor has it that Jerry has also been known to haunt the local streams and rivers with fly rod in hand.

For more information about his photography, Jerry can be reached at the following:

Phone: (541) 517-5937
E-mail: tbmphotog@yahoo.com
Web: http://www.jgowinsphoto.com

Jay Houston's
THE ELK HUNTER SERIES™

COMING OCTOBER 2006

A NEW INSTRUCTIONAL DVD SERIES ON HOW TO BECOME A MORE SUCCESSFUL ELK HUNTER

Available from ElkCamp.com
And
Major Retailers Everywhere

VOLUME ONE

PLANNING FOR A SUCCESSFUL HUNT

THE OUTFITTER NETWORK™
Coming 2007

"One Source Unlimited Solutions"
**BIG GAME HUNTING   TROPHY HUNTING
DANGEROUS GAME**

North America	Canada	South America
Africa	New Zealand	Asia
Elk	Mule Deer	Whitetail Deer
Black Bear	Brown Bear	Grizzly
Mountain Goat	Sheep	Mountain Lion
Caribou	Moose	Musk Ox
Wolf	Turkey	Polar Bear
Tarr	Chamois	Red Deer Stag
Kudu	Gemsbok	Blesbuck
Springbuck	Blue Wildebeest	Impala
Brindled Gnu	Baboon	Duiker
Warthog	Rock Hyrax	Nyala

www.theOutfitterNetwork.com

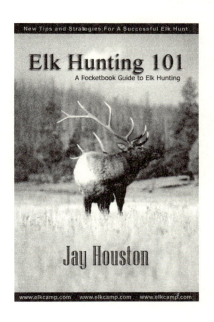

Elk Hunting 101

FASTEST SELLING BOOK ON ELK HUNTING 2004

Available at:
www.elkcamp.com
And major retailers

Elk Hunting 201

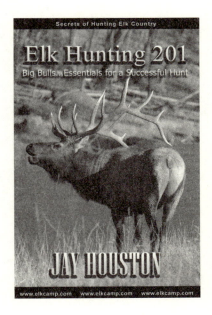

FASTEST SELLING BOOK ON ELK HUNTING 2005

Available at:
www.elkcamp.com
And major retailers

Elk Hunting Notes

Elk Hunting Notes

Elk Hunting Notes